Running
COLORADO'S FRONT RANGE

796.4

BY BRIAN METZLER
FOUNDING EDITOR OF *TRAIL RUNNER MAGAZINE*

MOUNTAIN SPORTS PRESS

Boulder, Colorado USA

Running Colorado's Front Range

Published by Mountain Sports Press

Distributed to the book trade by
PUBLISHERS GROUP WEST

Copyright © 2003 Brian Metzler

Bill Grout, Editor-in-Chief
Michelle Klammer Schrantz, Art Director
Scott Kronberg, Associate Art Director
Chris Salt, Managing Editor
Andy Hawk, Account Manager

Cover photo by: Phil Mislinski

ISBN 0-9717748-9-7
Library of Congress Cataloging-in-Publication Data applied for.

First paperback edition. June 2003

Printed in the USA, by RR Donnelley Corporation

For questions and comments, send an email to brian@coloradorunningguide.com

Table of Contents

Acknowledgements

To Mom and Dad
  Thank you for a lifetime of love and inspiration.

  A special thanks go out to my wife, Pamalyn Simich, for learning to love trail running as much as I do; my brother, Don Metzler, who could always run like the wind; training partners Mark Ruscin, Beth Reece, Jason Smith, Kevin Reinsch and Scott Boulbol, for a lifetime of epic runs; Monique Cole, Phil Mislinski and Boulbol, for their writing about running in Colorado; Michael Sandrock, for his incredible writing about competitive running; and my dog, Boggs, for always wanting to run with me, anytime, anywhere, rain or shine.

  Many thanks to the following Colorado runners for providing an inspiring exam-ple: high-altitude trail stalwart Matt Carpenter; 2000 U.S. Olympian Adam Goucher; world champion marathoner Mark Plaatjes; snowshoe- and trail-running phenom Anita Ortiz; CU's men's and women's cross-country teams and their coach, Mark Wetmore; adventure-running guru Buzz Burrell; and ultradistance trail runners Darcy Piceu, Dave Mackey, Bob Africa, Paul Pomeroy, Peter Bakwin, Peter Downing and Stephanie Ehret, among others. A big thank you also goes out to the many friends who provided additional encouragement for this book, including Megan and Craig Penn, Lisa Jhung, Mark Eller, Barry Siff and Sally Murdoch. Additional thanks goes out to the entire crew at the Boulder Running Company.

  This book wouldn't have been published without the vision and hard work of Andy Clurman, Bill Grout, Michelle Schrantz, Scott Kronberg, Natalie Kurylko and Paul Prince at Mountain Sports Media.

—Brian Metzler

Foreword

It's springtime in Colorado, and there is no place else I would rather be. The mercury has risen to the mid-70s during the past week, days are longer and the spring snow that blanketed Boulder's legendary trail system is melting in the bright Colorado sun. Motivations are high, races are breaking out each weekend and the possibility for another extraordinary running season abounds. So what the heck are you going to do about it? For starters, you need to open your wallet and buy this book as soon as you finish reading my foreword. I've checked many Colorado trail guides, but this one, by endurance sports journalist Brian Metzler, is the first that will truly allow you to get a grip on the running scene along Colorado's Front Range. It's unquestionably the best resource a runner could have, whether you've lived here for 20 years or just relocated from somewhere else.

Whatever your specific running goals or racing persuasions, running the countless trails and paths of Colorado's Front Range is as good as it gets. From the towering heights of Barr Trail in Manitou Springs and the ever-rolling Mesa Trail in Boulder to the more relaxed Highline Canal Trail in Denver, you have access to some of our country's finest state and municipal trail systems, not to mention some of the world's most fantastic topography and scenery. This book points out great places to do fast workouts, hill climbs and long, slow Sunday runs. It highlights the best races, running stores and coaches, and provides insightful tips and inspirational profiles of some of the region's best runners. It's a one-stop shop for runners who want to run a fast 10k or marathon, leave reality behind on the trails or shed the extra 15 pounds gained from devouring too many Carl's Jr. burgers and Taco Bell Chalupas during the winter.

As an elite middle-distance runner and trail athlete (admittedly a dubious combination), I thrive on experiencing the diverse opportunities that the Front Range offers. During one memorable season, I burned up the Boulder tarmac in the wicked Downhill 1k race and then suffered through the altitudinous agony of the notorious Pikes Peak Marathon two months later. This season finds me gearing up for several track races in May and then making the stark transition to the San Juan Solstice 50-mile trail race in late June. And that's the real beauty of what the Front Range affords runners: You can do it all!

Now that this book is in your hands, the fun is about to begin. Enjoy the best running season of your life.

—Jason Smith
2001 Pikes Peak Marathon Champion, 20-29 Age Group

Paul Pomeroy returns to the Chautauqua trailhead in Boulder after running to the 8,144-foot summit of Green Mountain.

Introduction

Running Colorado's Front Range

When I moved to Colorado from the Chicago area more than a decade ago, I was a frustrated runner. I was bored with 5k's and 10k's, not interested in running road marathons and too slow to be competitive on the track. So when I landed in Boulder, I decided I'd spend my time pursuing other passions—skiing, mountain biking, rock climbing, snowboarding, hiking and kayaking.

Three months after my arrival, I caught the bug again and went for a run on Boulder's Mesa Trail. I was not only energized for the entire 55-minute run, but the spirit of my off-road adventure almost immediately revitalized my passion for running. I started training like a fiend, ran the trails in and around Boulder daily (and sometimes twice daily). I ran my first Bolder Boulder 10k that spring and a dozen more Colorado races that summer. Along the way, I realized what an extraordinary place Colorado's Front Range can be for a runner.

Colorado's spectacular trails and wide variety of trail races inspired me in my role as founding editor-in-chief of *Trail Runner* magazine in 1999. The motivation for this book came partially from 10 incredible years of running in Colorado—on urban and wilderness trails, in Front Range road races, community track meets and ultradistance trail races and the spectacular 170-mile Colorado Relay.

Dozens of elite Colorado runners have also inspired me, everyone from high-altitude trail runner Matt Carpenter of Manitou Springs to former University of Colorado standout and 2000 track Olympian Adam Goucher. But the biggest stimulus for writing this guide came from the thousands of nameless runners I encountered while doing the research for this book. Seeing runners of all ages and abilities on a daily basis reinforced the notion that a book like this could come in very handy to a lot of people.

I've been fortunate enough to have the opportunity to have run in 32 states and seven countries, but most of my favorite places to run can be found in Colorado. Running through the jungles of Costa Rica, in the mountains of British Columbia and the coastlines of Hawaii are out-of-this-world experiences. But doing the research for this book reminded me how lucky we are to be able to run at so many incredible places along the Front Range on a weekly basis.

Whether you've just moved to Colorado or you've been running here for a long time, I hope this book will help you find some special places of your own.

Happy Trails,
Brian Metzler
Boulder, Colorado

How to use this book

The running routes in this book are organized into five major geographical sections: Front Range South (Colorado Springs, Manitou Springs and Pueblo), Denver Metro, Front Range West (Golden, Morrison, Evergreen, Idaho Springs, Lakewood and Littleton), Boulder and Front Range North (Fort Collins, Loveland, Longmont, Greeley and Estes Park). Each trail report features a detailed description with distances, trailhead locations and ratings for difficulty and elevation change, as well as a map and other running-related information. Each report also includes details about dog regulations, weather, wildlife and alternate routes.

The difficulty ratings for the routes selected vary between easy, moderate and hard. Make no mistake about it—the hard routes are difficult! If you're not accustomed to running uphill, at higher altitudes and/or on technical terrain for long periods of time, you might want to stick to routes with moderate or easy ratings. Moderate routes have occasional hills and other challenges, while easy routes are generally flat from start to finish.

Every route listed in this book is 100 percent runnable, although trails that earned an extreme rating for elevation change might require walking at times, depending on your fitness level and running ability. A minimal rating for elevation change means there is virtually no change on a route, while a moderate designation means you might be in for some hill climbing.

Each trail description includes specific dog regulations and an indication of whether or not a route is suitable for a running stroller. Always double-check trailhead signs to see if any dog-related rules have changed.

Front Range Run Locations

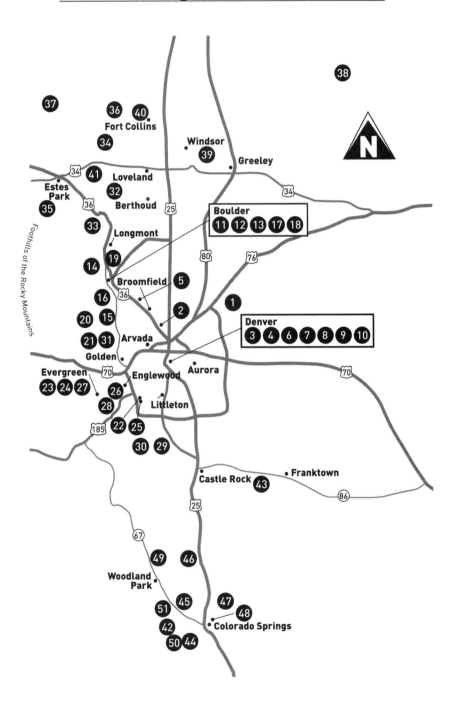

Key to the Maps

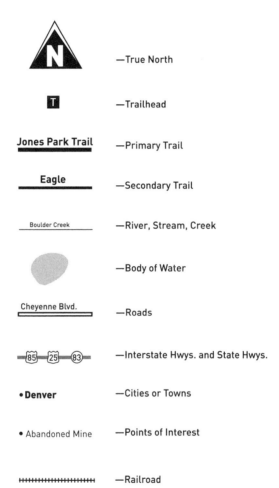

—True North

—Trailhead

Jones Park Trail —Primary Trail

Eagle —Secondary Trail

Boulder Creek —River, Stream, Creek

—Body of Water

Cheyenne Blvd. —Roads

—Interstate Hwys. and State Hwys.

•**Denver** —Cities or Towns

• Abandoned Mine —Points of Interest

—Railroad

Lisa Jhung is all smiles on this early morning run on East Boulder Trail.

Colorado's Front Range: A Runner's Paradise

Leave No Trace

This book encourages runners to follow the low-impact environmental ethics of Leave No Trace, a national nonprofit organization dedicated to promoting and inspiring outdoor recreation through education, research and partnerships. The basic principles of Leave No Trace include planning ahead, traveling on durable surfaces (and not fragile plant life), properly disposing of waste, leaving what you find, respecting wildlife and being considerate of others.

In other words, take only pictures and leave only footprints. While runners aren't typically known as litterbugs, every now and then you'll see an empty energy gel packet flattened on the side of a trail. Be sure you tuck your wrappers in a secure pocket so they don't wind up on the trail. Also, stay on designated trails at all times to prevent erosion, avoid trampling fragile plant life and keep from getting lost.

Dirt trails along the Front Range can often be muddy in the winter, spring and fall. To help prevent erosion, vegetation problems and the unnecessary widening of trails, Leave No Trace recommends staying on the trail and running straight through the mud.

For more information about Leave No Trace, visit www.LNT.org.

Trail Running Versus Road Running

Although running on roads and bike paths in urban areas and running on trails in the foothills both require running, the two activities are about as different as road cycling and mountain biking. Road running is usually an urban adventure that requires dodging traffic, waiting at stoplights and running on paved or concrete surfaces. Trail running means getting away from the "real world" for a while and escaping into sheer bliss, even if the trail is in the heart of an urban area like Denver's Highline Canal Trail.

When you're trail running, especially on wild and semi-wild trails in the foothills, you're usually running on dirt, gravel, pine needles or some other relatively soft surface. It also means you'll have a greater chance of encountering wildlife and some change in the weather. Most trail runners wear a waist pack to carry water, energy bars and additional clothing. (See the "Equipment and Apparel" section later in this chapter.) This book profiles a variety of running routes between Colorado Springs and Fort Collins, ranging from singletrack dirt trails to concrete bike paths. Knowing what to expect on each route will make your running experience better, regardless of ability level.

Safety

There are plenty of safety issues to adhere to while running, regardless of the route you've chosen. The following are a few points to consider before you head out for a run.

• Many urban routes profiled in this book include uncontrolled road crossings where you'll have to negotiate traffic before continuing your run on the other side of the road. Be extra careful (especially at night!) and don't jet out quickly just for the sake of preserving the continuity of your run. Drivers won't always be able to see you on the side of the road, nor will they expect you to run out in front of them.

• When you park your car to start a run, be sure not to leave any valuables in sight. Several communities have experienced a rash of trailhead break-ins in recent years. Store watches, cameras, wallets, cell phones, compact discs and other important items in the glove compartment or out of sight under a jacket.

• Getting lost is a good way to ruin a good trail run. Before you head out on a run, tell someone where you're going and double-check your route on appropriate maps and trailhead signage. If you're running a new trail, try to remember significant landmarks as you run—a big rock, an overhanging tree or a bridge over a stream. If you come to a trail junction, make mental notes of the surroundings so you'll know how to recognize it when you return. If you think you are lost, stay on trails at all times and try to backtrack your steps. When possible, follow trails downhill or downstream. If you still can't find your way back, reduce your speed to a walk and make sure to hydrate and stay warm.

Hydration

Whether you're running on a paved bike path in Denver or a technical singletrack trail in the foothills of Fort Collins, you should be hydrating early and often. The physical exertion of running, combined with Colorado's dry climate, can dehydrate your body even if you drank a tall glass of water before your run. As a rule of thumb, you should drink four ounces of water or sports drink for every 15 minutes of exercise. That means on a one-hour run, you should be carrying a least one full 16-ounce water bottle with you. (See the "Equipment and Apparel" section below.) At all times before, during and after a run or race, your body should be producing copious amounts of clear urine. If not, it's a sign that you're not optimally hydrated.

Rehydrating during a run is especially important when you're running at higher altitudes or running longer than an hour. Moderate dehydration can lead to muscle cramps, breathing difficulties, exhaustion, headaches and disorientation, while severe dehydration can lead to more serious health problems.

Because a variety of unknown contaminants might be lurking in the water, it's not wise to drink out of rivers, streams, ponds or lakes. The parasitical protozoan known as giardia is the most common problem, one that can lead to cramping, diarrhea and other ailments. Symptoms can set in from a day to a month after ingesting giardia, and they're always nasty. Some bacterial and viral pathogens can be removed with portable filters and purifiers or killed with iodine tablets, but it's much easier to carry your own water or arrange a run where you can refill your bottle or hydration pack with potable water.

Running at High Altitude

This book features several trails that top 9,000 feet above sea level. Running at high altitude can be difficult for anyone, regardless of fitness level, running skills or genetic make-up. Here are a few simple tips to ease the difficulty of running up high: (1) Start your runs considerably slower than you normally would on a run in the 5,000- to 6,000-foot range common to the cities along the Front Range, and run conservatively; if you run too hard early, you could have trouble finishing the route. (2) Dress slightly warmer than you think you should at the trailhead; conditions are bound to change and temperatures can drop rapidly in a short time. (3) Hydrate early and often; you're more likely to get dehydrated at high elevations. (4) Pack some kind of snack, such as an energy bar or a piece of fruit; it's easy to bonk up high, but a few quick calories can usually help stave off dizziness and other problems. (5) Wear a heart-rate monitor to see how hard your heart is really working; with the help of a coach, you can determine your specific heart-rate threshold for efficient training at altitude. (6) Remember to stop and enjoy the scenery every now and then; after all, that's the real reason you're there.

Equipment and Apparel

If you've lived in Colorado for a while, you've probably heard someone say: "If you don't like the weather in Colorado, don't worry—it will change." It's true, but it can play havoc with runners. It might be sunny and clear when you begin a run, but halfway into it you might feel a chilly wind on your face and raindrops on your head. Remember, it snows almost every month in Colorado at higher elevations.

• Because of the ever-changing environment in the foothills, it's wise to carry water (either in a hand-held bottle or some type of hydration pack), an energy gel or bar and perhaps an extra layer of clothing and light gloves for any run longer than 45 to 60 minutes. If nothing else, tie a long-sleeve shirt around your waist and carry a water bottle. That's especially true if you're running on wilderness trails at higher elevations or if you're running a trail for the first time. You never know when a summer storm will bring rain, chilly temperatures or snow. You should never head out on a long mountain run (90 minutes or longer) without a pack filled with the necessary extras.

• If you're not used to carrying water on your runs, a hydration pack might take some getting used to. Hydration packs range in price from about $35 to $100 and can be found at any Front Range running shop or outdoors store. Hydration packs generally come in two styles: waist packs with 30 to 50 ounces of fluid capacity or over-the-shoulder packs with 50 to 100 ounces of fluid capacity.

One of the best waist packs for trail running is CamelBak's FlashFlo ($40), which has a 45-ounce bladder and pockets large enough to hold your keys, energy bars and even a long-sleeve T-shirt or lightweight shell jacket. Boulder-based Go-Lite also makes a good fanny pack called the Hare ($49). One of the best over-the-shoulder packs for trail running and ultrarunning is Ultimate Direction's Endorfun ($75), which can carry as much as 96 ounces of water. (But don't try to run with more than about 60 ounces of water unless you're used to carrying big loads; 70 to 100 ounces of water can feel like a ton of bricks on your back once you get moving in the mountains.)

• Make sure you have the correct kind of running shoes for the surface on which you'll be running. While some shoes are versatile enough to wear on a variety of routes, it's certainly not true for most shoes. If you're running on concrete bike paths or roads, you'll want a lightweight, well-cushioned shoe designed for road running.

But if you're running a technical trail strewn with roots, rocks, gravel and other debris, it would be wise to get a pair of trail runners designed specifically for those obstacles. Trail running shoes offer built-in safety features like protective toe caps, protection plates to avoid push-through "stingers" (caused from sharp rocks or roots poking the bottom of your feet) and knobby outsoles for greater traction. Generally, trail shoes also have less cushioning so you can "feel" the trail and maneuver accordingly.

Running shoes range from $65 to $120; while you can save a few bucks by not buying a high-end model, you'll get what you pay for. The added features of the higher-priced models might be able to help you avoid injuries. Getting a proper fit should be your top priority. Your best bet is to visit one of the running retail stores listed in this book and to try on several pairs at the direction of the store's shoe-fitting experts.

• If you're still wearing cotton T-shirts when you run, you should consider joining the 21st century. Shirts made from moisture-wicking fabrics are not only lightweight and quick-drying, but they also pull moisture away from your skin and help reduce chaffing. A sweat-logged cotton shirt can chafe your skin and also leave you chilled if the weather changes or the sun ducks behind a cloud. In addition to moisture-wicking base layers, ultralight shell jackets and vests can also come in handy while running Colorado's Front Range. Both are made of water-resistant, windproof nylon that keep you just warm enough without letting you overheat.

• Running after dark can be either a joy or a necessity, depending on your daily schedule. Either way, it can be made easier with a lightweight running-specific headlamp. The newest models, made by companies such as Black Diamond, Essential Gear, Petzl, TSL and Princeton Tec, weigh less than five ounces with batteries and use high-intensity LEDs, arrays of multiple LED bulbs or a combination of LED and halogen lights. Superlight models with only one to three LED bulbs usually aren't bright enough to light up technical trails, but they're fine for running on roads, bike paths and smooth, groomed trails. Running headlamps cost between $30 and $75 and are available at most running shops and outdoor stores.

• Don't forget the sun block! Colorado's Front Range has more than 300 sunny days every year, which means during the majority of your runs, a portion of your skin will be exposed to the sun.

Dogs

If you are a dog owner (like me) and enjoy running with your dog (like me), please remember that not everyone shares that same joy. For that reason, please follow dog regulations for every trail and *always* be sure to pick up after your pooch. Many trailheads offer free bags to pick up your dog's poop, but that means you have to pack it with you and put it in a garbage can at the trailhead. Just don't follow the Boulder example: For some reason, many dog owners in Boulder bag their dog's dung but leave it on the trail as if someone else might pick it up for them. "There is a very strong belief in Boulder about a poop fairy that wanders around picking up bags of poop on the trails," says Dean Paschall, visitor and environmental services division manager for the Boulder Open Space and Mountain Parks Department. He's kidding—there is no poop fairy.

Dog regulations differ between communities and land agencies along the Front Range, so be sure to read the signage at the trailhead before heading out. Typically, there are three categories of laws: (1) no dogs allowed; (2) dogs must remain on a six-foot leash at all times; and (3) dogs are allowed off-leash but must be under voice and sight control at all times. (Train your dog to run on trail and curtail its instinct for chasing wildlife—especially prairie dogs—or livestock.)

If you think you won't get caught, think again! Rangers patrol the trails and write $50 to $75 tickets on a regular basis. While researching this book, I witnessed a ranger with the Jefferson County Open Space Department using a pair of binoculars to watch runners and hikers with dogs. In one instance, a runner returned with the dog on-leash but was written a warning because the ranger had seen the dog off-leash in his specs. If you're lucky, you might get away with a warning. But keep in mind that if a particular land agency receives a rash of complaints about dogs, it could eventually lead to changes in dog regulations. For example, Boulder's Mountain Parks and Open Space Department has limited dog accessibility and tightened leash laws in recent years. In a worst-case scenario, if your dog bites someone while off-leash you could be handed a $1,000 fine and the opportunity to spend 90 days in jail.

If you are going to run with your dog, keep in mind that your pooch will need water and snacks on long runs just as you do. Be careful not to run your dog too far, too soon. Most veterinarians recommend ramping up your dog's mileage slowly. While some breeds can run for five or six hours without any trouble at all, others will tire after an hour. If your dog lags behind and starts sitting down on the trail, it's a sign that it's well beyond its limit. At that point, you should curtail your run and treat Fido to a warm bath and a massage later that night.

For more tips about running with your dog, contact the American Dog Owners Association at (518) 477-8468.

Other Trail Users

Although you might feel a new element of freedom while running on trails and bike paths, very rarely will you be the only one on that route. Mountain bikers, road cyclists, walkers, hikers and horseback riders are among the other frequent users on most of the trails listed in this book, but you'll also have to keep your eyes peeled for dogs, kids on skateboards and scooters and a variety of baby strollers. In other words, keep your eyes open, be courteous and run defensively. Get ready to jump out of the way in a split second to avoid getting "Schwinned" by an oncoming biker or trampled by an oncoming horse. Generally, horses always have the right of way. If you come upon a horse, it's wise to stop running and step off the trail to let it pass without being spooked. Acknowledge the rider, especially if you approach from behind. Otherwise, yield to all uphill trail users (hikers, runners and mountain bikers) but be cautious in all situations. Don't expect everyone to know trail etiquette and make room for you.

Wildlife

One of the best aspects of running in Colorado is the potential for seeing wild animals in their natural habitat. But an encounter with a wild animal could be dangerous, especially for a trail runner. Most of the running routes in this book wind through the habitat of some kind of wildlife, including deer, foxes, snakes, coyotes, skunks, raptors, bears and mountain lions. These animals will typically not bother you unless they are startled or feel threatened.

While many animals could potentially do you harm, the most troublesome encounters with wildlife in Colorado are with snakes, bears and mountain lions. While pepper spray and mace can help keep aggressive animals at bay, they can also antagonize a predator and put you even further in harm's way.

• Although you should try to avoid all snakes, the only snakes you need worry about are rattlesnakes. But typically when you encounter a snake it's too late to discern what type it is. If you encounter a slithering serpent, back away slowly and give it space to continue on its way. If it's a rattlesnake, get yourself (and your dog) out of striking distance immediately. Don't antagonize a snake or try to move it from the trail under any circumstances.

• Sightings of black bears are common in the foothills of the Front Range, especially during droughts, when food is hard to find. Black bears are very agile and can run in bursts up to 35 miles an hour. They're good tree climbers and excellent swimmers. In other words, if you see a bear, don't bother running away; the bear is a much better trail runner than you, even without fancy shoes. Running at dawn or dusk may increase your chances of meeting bear, so it's wise to run with a partner at those times.

If you encounter a black bear in the woods, don't panic. Reduce your run to a walk and then slowly back away from the area. As you move away, talk out loud to make sure the bear is aware of your presence. Avoid direct eye contact with the animal, so as not to threaten it. Wild bears very rarely attack people unless they feel threatened or provoked. If the bear stands upright, it might be trying to detect smells in the air. Once it determines you're not a threat, it may leave the area or try to intimidate you by charging at you. If the bear attacks, you must fight back with a stick, rocks, hydration pack or even your bare hands. More than likely, the bear will sense that you're a fit athlete and retreat at once.

• Meeting a mountain lion on a trail could be deadly, especially if it's a mother protecting her young. Several people have been attacked by mountain lions in the past 100 years, and two have died as a result. Furthermore, the quick movements of a runner can make a lion defensive or even prompt an attack. If you see a mountain lion while running, stop immediately and calmly back away so as to leave the lion room to escape. Do whatever you can to make yourself look as large as possible, either by raising your arms or by grabbing a stick or branch. If the lion approaches or attacks, fight back by throwing rocks, sticks and branches and call out for help. Never crouch down in the presence of a lion, and never turn your back.

Mark Ruscin and Robert Page take time out for an afternoon run around Ferril Lake in Denver's City Park.

Denver Metro Area

T he Mile High City is known for a lot of things—Lower Downtown, the Denver Broncos, the Great Western Stock Show—but it usually doesn't make the cut when national running magazines publish lists of the top running cities in the U.S.

Still, Denver and its close-in suburbs have a rabid running population and dozens of good unpaved running trails hidden in its urban mayhem. Although it hasn't had much luck developing a major metro marathon, Denver and the surrounding towns host more than 100 road and trail running races every year.

"I can't think of any community anywhere that is as blessed with so many running trails as we have in the Denver metro area," says Creigh Kelley, a longtime Denver-area runner, race director and running shoe retailer. "There are so many great places to run. We're really pretty spoiled."

So, forget what those hokey lists say—Denver is a city on the run.

Barr Lake State Park Run 1

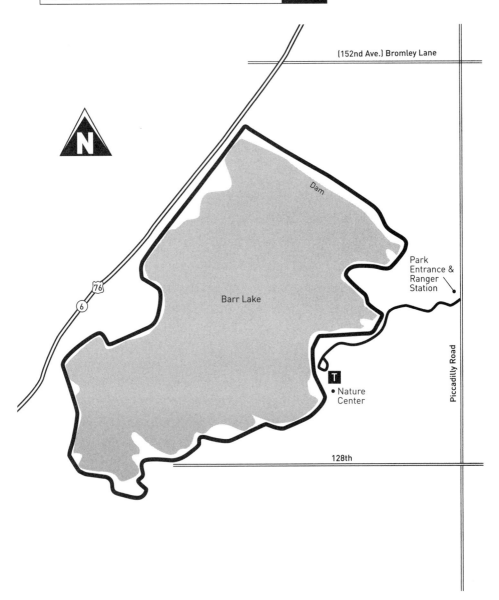

(152nd Ave.) Bromley Lane

Dam

Park
Entrance &
Ranger
Station

Barr Lake

Piccadilly Road

T
● Nature
Center

76
6

128th

Barr Lake State Park (Brighton)
Run 1

Distance/Terrain: An 8.5-mile loop on wide, dirt trails.

Difficulty: Easy.

Elevation Change: Minimal. This loop is as flat as a pancake.

Trailhead: The main park entrance is off of Piccadilly Road north of 128th Street, in Brighton. Once inside the park, follow the road to the nature center and park in the main parking area. Note: The park charges an entrance fee of $6 per vehicle.

Dogs: Canines are allowed in the park but must be leashed. Dogs are prohibited from entering the wildlife refuge on the south end of the lake but are allowed on the entire perimeter trail.

Running Strollers: Sure, but off-road models will do much better than traditional baby joggers built for pavement.

Route Description: Barr Lake State Park is a tranquil sanctuary for wildlife, bird watchers and trail runners alike. The 2,715-acre park includes a 1,900-acre reservoir, numerous marshes, several cottonwood groves and one of the metro area's largest wildlife refuges. It's a great place to run fast or slow, as it is rarely crowded and only occasionally windy.

The 8.8-mile loop around the reservoir and marsh is simple and very peaceful. Starting from the nature center in a clockwise direction, the dirt trail follows the historic Denver & Hudson Canal, one of several irrigation ditches that transport water to the farmlands in northeastern Colorado. The trail passes two popular bird-watching areas and then turns around the south end of the loop.

On the eastern side of the lake, it passes near Barr Lake Village RV Park (mile 4.0) and then continues in a northeasterly direction for 1.5 miles before taking a hard right turn at the historic Bruderlin Stone House—a farmhouse built in 1889 by Swiss immigrant Emil Bruderlin. From there, the trail dips down below a dam on the northwest side of the lake and continues for 1.5 miles southeast before taking a right and shadowing the zigzagging Denver & Hudson Canal for the final 1.5 miles back to the nature center. (Note: A 4.7-mile section of the loop on the back side of the lake is closed one hour past sunset until one hour prior to sunrise so as not to disturb the wildlife in the area.)

Wildlife: Deer, raccoons, squirrels, foxes, coyotes, a variety of snakes, more than 350 species of birds (including hawks, owls and eagles) and a wide variety of

Which way are you headed? This signpost at Barr Lake State Park gives you plenty
of options.

fish (trout, walleye, muskie and bass) in the reservoir. In recent years, the park has been the site of one of the only bald eagle nests in the Denver metro area.

Weather: The loop is susceptible to high winds, especially on the west side of the lake. In the spring, parts of the trail can be very muddy. Although trees surround the trail, there isn't much shelter from rainstorms.

Other Users: Walkers, bicyclists, horseback riders and gaggles of bird watchers.

Map: Barr Lake State Park Map, Colorado State Parks.

Contact Info: (303) 659-6005, www.parks.state.co.us.

Big Dry Creek Trail (Westminster)
Run 2

Distance/Terrain: Up to 9.0 miles (one way) on wide dirt and gravel trails and concrete bike paths.

Difficulty: Easy. The entire route is flat and smooth.

Elevation Change: Minimal. The route contains a few minor rolling hills.

Trailheads: There are several places to access Big Dry Creek Trail, including the North Standley Lake Open Space, City Park, Front Range Community College and the eastern terminus near 128th Street and Huron.

Dogs: Your pooch is allowed but must be leashed at all times.

Running Strollers: Yes, the smooth surfaces of this trail are perfect for suburban stroller pushers.

Route Description: Westminster is one of the many cities along Colorado's Front Range that has exploded out of vacant rolling fields. The urban sprawl is unfortunate, but at least city planners made sure to set aside land for Big Dry Creek Trail. It's too bad much of the trail is made of concrete, but it's still a good refuge for runners in an otherwise very congested community.

The trail follows Dry Creek as it winds through the city from Standley Lake to the northeast corner of the city limits near 128th Street and Huron. The trail starts at North Standley Lake Open Space Park, near Simms Street and West 100th Avenue. The route begins as a concrete path, but turns to a fine-gravel and dirt mix after about 1.0 mile as it follows the tree-lined Dry Creek drainage. After passing under busy Wadsworth Parkway and through a 75-foot tunnel underneath a railroad track (mile 2.0), you pop out on 99th Avenue at Ammons Circle. Go east three blocks along 99th Avenue, and you'll reach Wadsworth Boulevard and the

Big Dry Creek Trail `Run 2`

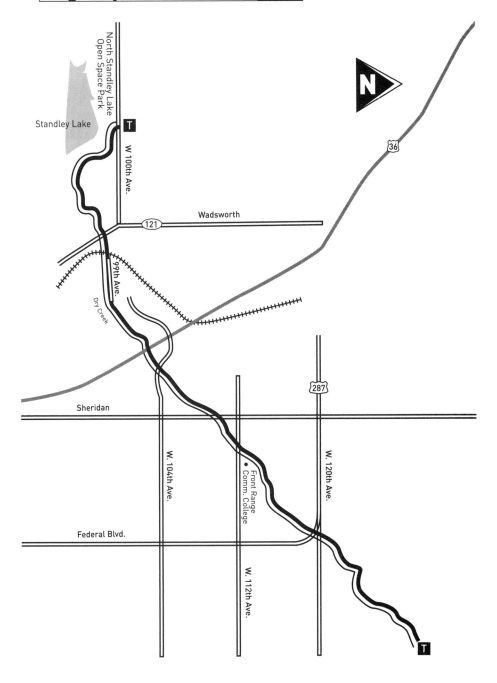

only road crossing on the entire trail. This portion of the route cuts through a surprisingly rural part of Westminster—keep your eyes peeled for several old barns, horse breeders and other signs of agriculture.

The trail turns into a concrete path again and swings around the Spring Hill Suites hotel, crosses over the creek on a short bridge, cuts through a tunnel under Highway 36 and into the Big Dry Creek Open Space behind the Butterfly Pavilion and Insect Center. Still a concrete path, it ducks under 104th Street and pops up in Westminster's massive but rarely crowded City Park (mile 4.0). To your right are several ball fields and a community center; to your left is a Westin Hotel with its finely manicured lawns and a faux tropical waterfall that look very out of place amid the arid surroundings. Take the large metal bridge to the north side of the creek and make an immediate right. After another 0.5 mile, cross back to the creek's south side, where the trail turns to gravel again after it passes under Sheridan Road (mile 5.0).

The trail crosses the creek again, passes under Dillon Road and winds up through the large open-space area behind Front Range Community College. More than two dozen species of birds inhabit the ponds, willows and grasslands in this area, but an even larger population of prairie dogs also claims this area as its own.

From here, the trail ducks under 120th Avenue (mile 7.0) and into a more residential area of the city. After 2.0 more miles, the path dead-ends near 128th and Huron. Plans are in the works to continue the trail under I-25, where it will connect with a trail system in Thornton.

Wildlife: Deer, raccoons, skunks, rabbits, geese, ducks, foxes, coyotes, snakes, and more than two dozen species of owls, raptors and other birds.
Weather: The route is accessible year-round. It's protected from the wind in many places, but it can be icy and snow-packed in winter.
Other Users: Bicyclists and walkers.
Map: City of Westminster Open Space Map, 2002.
Contact Info: City of Westminster, (303) 430-2400 ext. 2192, www.ci.westminster.co.us/website/Trails

Mark Ruscin revs up the motors on Big Dry Creek Trail in Westminster.

Cherry Creek Bikeway
(Denver/Aurora)
Run 3

Distance/Terrain: About 12.5 miles (one way) on wide, concrete bike paths.
Difficulty: Easy.
Elevation Change: Minimal. Only a few very gradual slopes are found on the
  entire route.
Trailheads: There are a few official trailheads, but virtually limitless access points
  along Cherry Creek. The most obvious places to start a run are from
  Confluence Park in Lower Downtown, Cherry Creek Shopping Center at 1st
  Avenue and University Boulevard, Garland Park or Cook Park on either side of
  Monaco Parkway, or Cherry Creek Reservoir in Englewood.
Dogs: Yes, dogs are allowed but must be on a leash at all times.
Running Strollers: The concrete path is perfect for running strollers.

Route Description: Cherry Creek Bike Path is a concrete trail that starts at
Confluence Park and meanders through the heart of Denver all the way to Cherry
Creek State Recreation Area, with only a few road crossings. It's an easily accessible urban getaway, whether for a quick lunchtime run or a long training workout
on the weekend. It's really a two-part route, with the northwestern section
between Lower Downtown and the Denver Country Club and the southeastern
part between the Cherry Creek Shopping Center and the state recreation area.
The southeastern section has a decidedly less urban flavor than the very struc-
tured northwestern end near the city.

Starting from Confluence Park, where Cherry Creek spills into the South
Platte River, Cherry Creek Bike Path follows a gully along Speer Boulevard from
Lower Downtown to the affluent residential neighborhoods near the Denver
Country Club and the Cherry Creek Shopping Center. In this 4.5-mile section, the
path and creek are sunken about 10 to 15 feet below street level, creating an ideal
conduit for uninterrupted urban running that is especially popular at lunchtime on
weekdays. In spring and summer, the submerged canyon formed by the concrete
and brick walls are lined with ivy, green grass and flowers. In winter, those same
walls help keep chilly winds at bay.

Unfortunately, the path abruptly ends near 1st Avenue and Downing Street as
the creek enters the grounds of the exclusive Denver Country Club. To continue
your run, follow the sidewalk along 1st Avenue until you reach University
Boulevard. Take a right on University and cross the boulevard at Cherry Creek

Cherry Creek Bikeway   Run 3

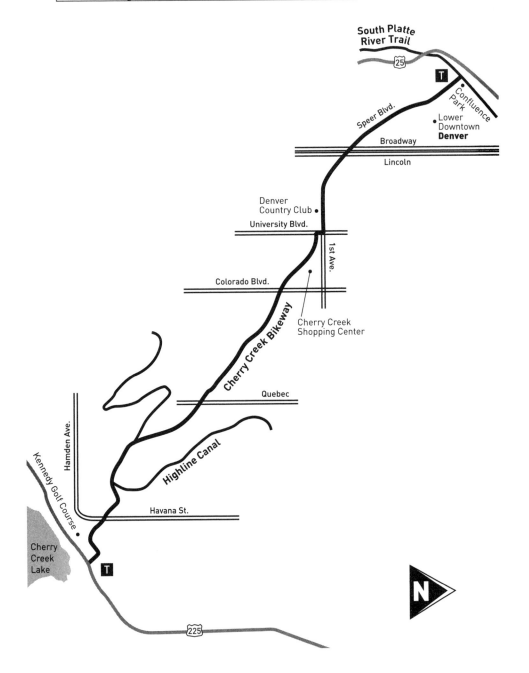

South Platte
River Trail

25

Speer Blvd.

Confluence
Park

Lower
Downtown
Denver

Broadway

Lincoln

Denver
Country Club

University Blvd.

1st Ave.

Colorado Blvd.

Cherry Creek
Shopping Center

Cherry Creek Bikeway

Quebec

Hamden Ave.

Highline Canal

Kennedy Golf Course

Havana St.

Cherry
Creek
Lake

225

N

The easily accessed Cherry Creek Bikeway is a peaceful escape from Denver's urban mayhem.

Drive. The bike path resumes on the north side of the road (as it passes Cherry Creek Shopping Center) and continues about 7.5 miles to Cherry Creek Reservoir, with only a few minor road crossings.

As it continues southeast, the trail picks up a much wilder atmosphere. Replacing the flower beds, manicured lawns and flow-control stream are an assortment of wild trees, tall native grasses, sandy creek banks and a lot more wildlife. After crossing under Steele Street and Colorado Boulevard, the path pops up to street level and passes through Four Mile Historic Park (the site of Denver's oldest home) and Garland Park along Cherry Creek Drive. Near Oneida Street, the path crosses a pedestrian bridge to the south side of the creek and continues the rest of the way without any road crossings.

Much of the remaining 4 miles of the route feature singletrack dirt trails that run adjacent to the main route, offering a break from the hard-pounding of the concrete. About 6 miles from the shopping center, Cherry Creek Bike Path intersects and actually shares a route with Highline Canal for about 0.5 mile before splitting again on the back side of Los Verdes Golf Club. The Cherry Creek path meanders through the John F. Kennedy Golf Course, dips under Havana Street, runs by more of the golf course and then dips under I-225 and into Cherry Creek State Recreation Area.

Alternate Routes: The Cherry Creek Bike Path connects to the South Platte River Greenway (see the "Platte River Trail" section on page 36) at Confluence Park and the Highline Canal Trail (see the section entitled "Highline Canal Trail Northeast" on page 31) in southeast Denver, making a variety of off-street ultra-distance runs possible.

Wildlife: Squirrels, foxes, raccoons, birds, raptors and deer.
Weather: The creek path is a popular place to run all year, but especially in the summer. It can be icy and snowy in the winter, and occasionally it can flood in the springtime.
Other Users: Cyclists, walkers and stroller pushers.
Map: Cherry Creek Bikeway Map, City and County Denver, Department of Parks and Recreation.
Contact Info: (303)331-4060, www.denvergov.org/parks.

City Park (Denver)
Run 4

Distance/Terrain: 2.0 to 4.0 miles (per loop) on paved trails and dirt paths.
Difficulty: Easy.
Elevation Change: Minimal.
Trailhead: Although the main entrance is on 17th Avenue just east of York Street, there are unlimited places to start your run in City Park. If you can't find parking at the main entrance, try a side street off of 17th Street on the south side of the park.
Dogs: Yes, dogs are allowed, but you've gotta keep 'em on a leash.
Running Strollers: Jogging strollers will work well on the park's paved roads, but not on the dirt social trail that borders the golf course.

Route Description: City Park was developed as Denver's cornerstone park in the early 1900s. The 314-acre park has a public golf course, tennis courts, flower gardens and two small lakes. Spectacular views of the mountains, including Mount Evans, are visible from the eastern edge of the park near the Denver Museum of Natural History.

City Park always seems to be much less crowded than Washington Park (see section later in the chapter), especially when it comes to running. Still, the 2.0-

City Park Run 4

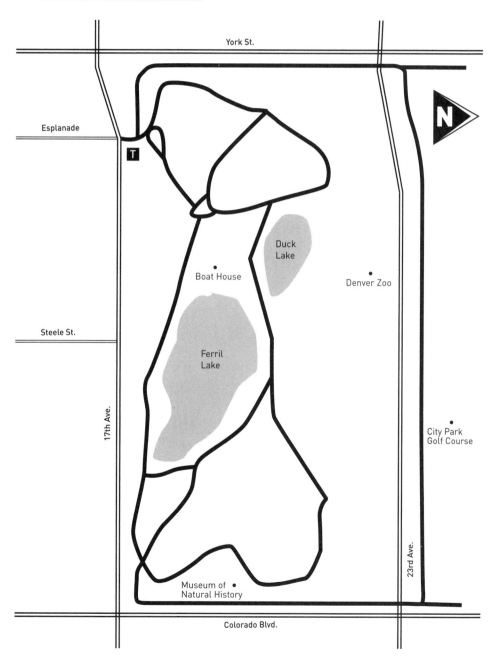

mile paved loop around Ferril Lake is adequate enough for short runs. There's not much to it, but it's a good place to do fartlek (interval) workouts, because there are no crowds, bikes and traffic to interrupt your run.

There are typically several races held in City Park every year, most of which are 5k events put on by BKB, a company that organizes races. Visit www.bkbltd.com for details.

Alternate Routes: The best way to maximize your running at City Park is to incorporate the dirt trails that run around the perimeter of the park and the adjacent city-operated golf course between 23rd and 26th streets and York Street and Colorado Boulevard. (But keep your eyes peeled for errant drives, and duck if you hear someone yelling "Fore!") The entire loop around the golf course is about 2.5 miles, while one big loop around the park and the golf course is close to 4.0 miles.

Wildlife: Ducks, geese, wild birds and an assortment of exotic animals—in the Denver Zoo, that is.

Weather: The park is accessible year-round and is typically not windy. A portion of the park roads and paths are plowed after big snowfalls in winter.

Other Users: Bicyclists, walkers, soccer players, golfers and usually dozens of people attending picnics or special events.

Map: City Park Map, City and County Denver, Department of Parks and Recreation.

Contact Info: (303) 370-6668; www.denvergov.org/parks.

Coal Creek Trail (Louisville/Lafayette)
Run 5

Distance/Terrain: 7.5 miles (one way) on wide gravel or dirt trails, concrete sidewalks and paved roads.

Difficulty: Easy.

Elevation Change: Minimal. The trail drops about 200 feet from the west terminus on McCaslin Blvd. in Superior to the ending point on 120th Street in Lafayette. There is only one semi-steep hill on the route, but it is short and very runnable.

Trailheads: Many access points, including McCaslin Blvd., the Coal Creek Golf Course parking lot, the Aquarius trailhead and several connecting parks and trails in Louisville and Lafayette. Because there are few places to park on the

Coal Creek Trail Run 5

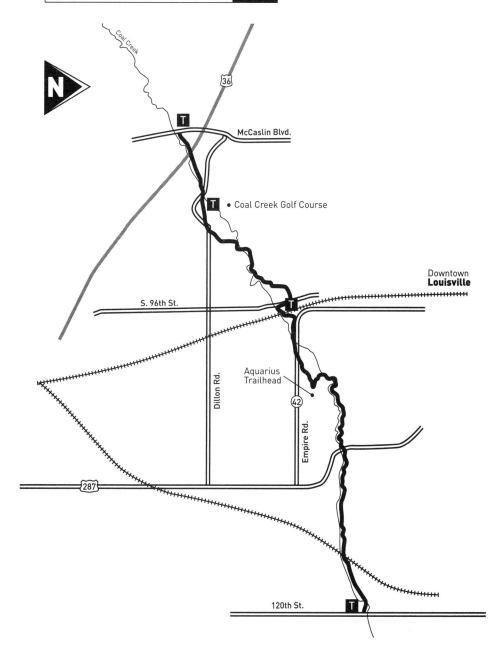

eastern section of the trail (and none at the trail's eastern terminus in Lafayette), it is wise to start this run from Louisville.

Dogs: Dogs are allowed but must be on leash at all times.

Running Strollers: Yes, the entire trail is conducive to strollers.

Route Description: A mostly flat, meandering route, the trail follows Coal Creek, from the south end of Louisville to the east side of Lafayette. Typically not crowded, it quietly sneaks past Coal Creek Golf Course, three active farms, several housing subdivisions and a few industrial areas. The creek is shrouded by a variety of deciduous trees and ground foliage that are home to a wide variety of wildlife. A portion of the trail that rises away from the creek offers great views of the Coal Creek Valley and the foothills in Boulder.

Starting from McCaslin Boulevard just south of the Highway 36 interchage, follow the trail north by northeast as it parallels Coal Creek. The trail ducks under Highway 36 and then under Dillon Road near the Coal Creek Golf Course. From there, it turns into a concrete sidewalk that winds through a housing subdivision. (The route is marked in places, but it's obvious where to run even without the signs.) After a mile or so, the sidewalks give way to a fine gravel path, skimming the eastern border of the golf course adjacent to Coal Creek. It crosses the creek and winds 1.3 miles to the outskirts of downtown Louisville. When the trail pops out on Aspen Way, make a right and then head north by making a left on Roosevelt Street. After about a mile, veer to the right across the open field (which will eventually become a Louisville city park) and look for the trailhead marker across the 96th Street next to the railroad crossing.

The trail continues to the south along the west side of the railroad tracks for about 0.25 mile, then cuts under a bridge and follows the creek toward Highway 42. After crossing under Highway 42, the trail encounters the only significant hill on the route. The trail rises slowly about 250 feet above the valley floor (passes the Aquarius trailhead) and then begins a quick drop that culminates (after crossing Empire Drive) alongside the creek.

From the Empire Drive crossing, the trail meanders alongside the creek for another 3.5 miles through Lafayette to the eastern terminus at 120th Street. Along the way, there is a bird sanctuary called Raptor Rapture, where several species of hawks can often be seen (rough-legged, red-tailed and Swainson's, to name a few), as well as kestrels, owls and an occasional bald eagle. You'll know you're near the trail's end when you cross to the south side of the creek and then pass underneath an old wooden railroad bridge.

Wildlife: Deer, squirrels, foxes, raccoons, hawks and maybe a bald eagle (if you're lucky).

Weather: The trail is accessible year-round, but it's not nearly as popular in the winter months. Although the trail is mostly gravel and dirt, it doesn't get too sloppy when it snows or rains.

Other Users: Cyclists, walkers and stroller pushers.

Maps: City of Louisville Open Space, City of Lafayette Open Space.

Contact Info: Louisville: (303)335-4735, www.ci.louisville.co.us/links.htm. Lafayette: (303)665-4206, www.cityoflafayette.com/parksrec.

Highline Canal Trail (Northeast)
(Denver/Aurora)
Run 6

Distance/Terrain: Up to 15 miles (one way) on wide concrete and asphalt bike paths.

Difficulty: Easy.

Elevation Change: Minimal. With the exception of a few gradual slopes in Aurora, the canal trail is virtually flat the entire route.

Trailheads: There are an unlimited number of places to start a run on the north-eastern section of the Highline Canal in Aurora, including Hinkley High School, Aurora Community College, Delaney Farm Open Space, City Center Park and Expo Park. Another good starting/ending point is James A. Bible Park in south-east Denver.

Dogs: Yes, but they must be on a leash at all times. There are many road crossings on this route, so be sure to keep dogs in check when crossing traffic.

Running Strollers: Yes, the majority of the trail is flat and paved.

Route Description: Completed in 1883, the 68-mile Highline Canal was built to provide water to communities throughout the Denver metro area. Nowadays, the adjacent pathways serve as ideal running trails for the residents of those communities. The northeastern section, which cuts through east Denver and Aurora, isn't as conducive to running as the rural southern section. Even during non-peak hours, running this route means a lot of stopping and starting at road crossings. Still, much of the route is off-street and shrouded by trees, which makes it much better than running on sidewalks or along busy roads.

One of the better starting points is Aurora Community College near First

Highline Canal Trail (Northeast) `Run 6`

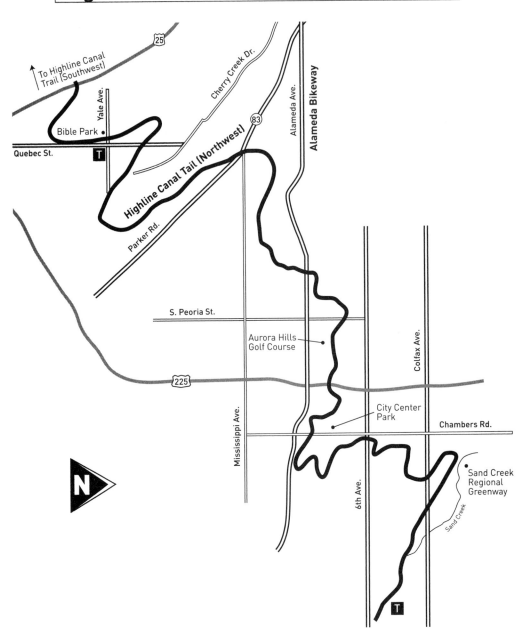

Avenue and Chambers Road. From there, the trail winds southward through Delaney Farm Open Space, ducks under busy Chambers Road and cuts around the back side of Aurora's city government buildings and library (mile 1.5).

The trail meanders through a residential area and cuts under I-225 along a sidewalk on Ellsworth Avenue. From there, it crosses Potomac Street (mile 3.0) and then meanders west along the north side of Aurora Hills Golf Course and a residential area for several miles. After turning southwest, the trail runs along Expo Park (mile 5.0), where it intersects with Westerly Creek Trail.

From there, Highline Canal Trail turns back west, crosses busy Havana Street and ducks into one of the more secluded portions of its northern section. Screened by trees as it passes through two quiet neighborhoods, it pops out and crosses Dayton Street, ducks back into the trees, skirts placid Windsor Lake and massive Fairmount Cemetery (mile 7.0), crosses Leetsdale Drive near Mississippi Avenue and heads south along Quebec Way.

The trail continues with a semi-secluded 3.0-mile stretch that has only two road crossings. When the route curves around Los Verdes Golf Club and crosses Cherry Creek (mile 10.5), it ties into and shares the same concrete path with Cherry Creek Bike Path (see entry above) for about a mile. After another 1.5 miles and a hairpin turn, the path reaches pastoral James A. Bible Park (mile 12.0).

Wildlife: Foxes, squirrels, possums, raccoons, snakes and lots of birds.
Weather: The trail is accessible year-round. In winter, portions of it are plowed after big snows, although they can still be icy at times.
Other Users: Lots of bicyclists and walkers.
Map: Denver Water Highline Canal Map, www.water.denver.co.gov/recreation/hilcnlmap.html.
Contact Info: Aurora City Parks and Open Space, (303) 739-7160; Denver Parks and Recreation Department, (303) 698-4903.

Highline Canal Trail (Southwest)
(Cherry Hills Village/Greenwood Village/Littleton)
Run 7

Distance/Terrain: About 10.0 miles (one way) on wide dirt and crushed-gravel trails and concrete bike paths.

Difficulty: Easy.

Elevation Change: Minimal.

Trailheads: Highline Canal's southeastern section has numerous access points, including Three Pond Park in Cherry Hills Village and Goodson Recreation Center in Littleton's deKoevend Park.

Dogs: Dogs are allowed, but must be on leash at all times.

Running Strollers: Yes, running strollers will work on these trails, but the off-road variety work better.

Route Description: Completed in 1883, the 68-mile Highline Canal was built to provide water to communities throughout the Denver metro area. Nowadays, the adjacent pathways serve as ideal running trails for the residents of those communities.

The southeastern section of Highline Canal Trail between Cherry Hills Village and the southern end of Littleton is the best running trail in the heart of Denver. Unlike the urban-flavored northeastern section in east Denver and Aurora, this leg has a much more pastoral vibe. It's a rural respite just minutes from the Denver Tech Center and Denver's crowded south suburbs.

Starting from Three Pond Park about one mile south of the intersection of Hampden Avenue and Colorado Boulevard in Cherry Hills Village, the soft-dirt and crushed-gravel trail meanders southward along the canal all the way to McLellan Reservoir. There are surprisingly few road crossings in the first few miles of this route, but plenty of sights to see—horse stables, wildlife refuge ponds, vast open fields and gargantuan upscale homes.

Belleview Avenue (mile 2.75) is the first major road crossing, and after another 0.5 mile or so, you'll turn due east, follow a 180-degree horseshoe turn and head due west for nearly a mile. After that, the trail goes south for another mile, turns to the west at a junction with Little Dry Creek Trail (mile 5.5) and parallels Orchard Road for a half mile.

By that point, the Highline Canal Trail is decidedly more suburban—more people, more road crossings and more modest-size homes on smaller lots. The trail continues

Highline Canal Trail (Southwest) Run 7

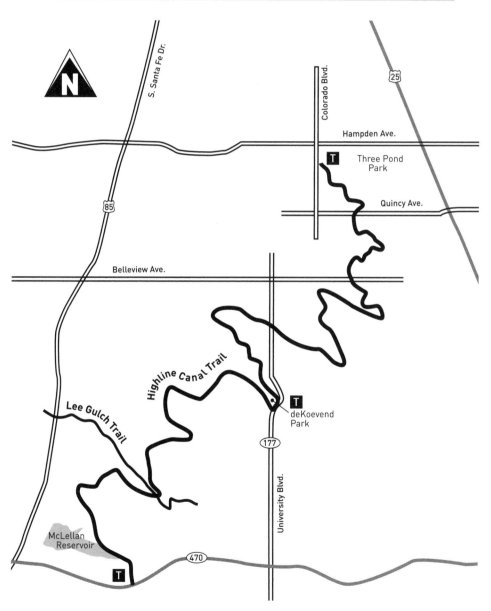

in a northwesterly direction for 2.0 miles, and after crossing University Boulevard, it suddenly bends back to the southwest. The trail ducks under Orchard Road and approaches deKoevend Park and the Goodson Recreation Center (mile 10.0)

Alternate Routes: From the Goodson Recreation Center, the Highline Canal Trail winds through deKoevend Park and zigzags its way southwest through Littleton's crowded residential areas. In fact, you can run all the way to Chatfield State Park, about 10 miles from the rec center. The trail varies between crushed gravel and concrete bike paths on this section, but there are numerous road crossings to negotiate.

Wildlife: Deer, foxes, coyotes, possums, raccoons, snakes, skunks, and a variety of birds.
Weather: The trail is accessible year-round and typically not muddy during winter and spring. Because tall deciduous and evergreen trees line the canal in most sections, the trail is often shady—especially in the morning.
Other Users: Bicyclists, walkers and stroller pushers.
Maps: South Suburban Parks and Recreation District Trail Map; Denver Water Highline Canal Map, www.water.denver.co.gov/recreation/hilcnlmap.html.
Contact Info: (303)798-5131, www.ssprd.org.

Platte River Trail (Denver/Littleton)
Run 8

Distance/Terrain: Up to 16 miles (one way) on wide, concrete bike paths.
Difficulty: Easy.
Elevation Change: Minimal. The trail has some minor dips and gullies, but overall it drops less than 200 feet from Denver to Littleton.
Trailheads: There are an unlimited number of places to start a run on the South Platte River Trail, including Confluence Park, Ruby Hill Park, Englewood Golf Course and The Hudson Gardens and Event Center.
Dogs: Yes, dogs are allowed but must be on a leash at all times.
Running Strollers: Yes, it's one of the best trails in the metro area for running strollers.

Route Description: One of the longest continuous trails in the metro area, the Platte River Trail runs (with few road crossings) from Confluence Park in the heart of Lower Downtown in Denver to Chatfield Reservoir in Littleton. (The trail also continues northeast toward the city of Brighton; see "Alternate Routes" below.)

Starting at Confluence Park, where Cherry Creek spills into the South Platte

The Cherry Creek Bikeway intersects with the Platte River Trail at Confluence Park in Denver.

River, the trail heads west along the railroad tracks of the Platte Valley Trolley. This part of the trail provides glimpses of some of the best recreation and entertainment venues in the Denver metro area, including kayaking in the river, Elitch Gardens amusement park, the Ocean Journey aquarium and Children's Museum. About a mile down the path on the right is Invesco Field (otherwise known as Mile High Stadium), home of the Denver Broncos and the Colorado Rapids.

The trail turns to the southeast and continues for 3.0 miles, alternating between industrial settings and pocket parks. At about mile 4.5, the trail and the river turn to the south and roughly follow Santa Fe Drive. As the trail splits from the road and cuts through Overland Park and Ruby Hill Park, mountains become visible on the western horizon. At mile 8.5, the South Platte River Trail crosses under Hampden Avenue, ties into Bear Creek Trail (see "Bear Creek State Park ," in the Front Range West chapter) and continues by crossing the river at the north side of Englewood Golf Course.

From there, the trail meanders along the edge of the golf course and continues past several junkyards and dirty broken-down buildings. But the scenery eventually changes for the better as the trail passes Centennial Golf Course and Tennis Center. The tree-lined trail splits into two legs as it passes under Bowles Avenue (mile 12.0), but the legs reunite within about 0.5 mile.

The Platte River Trail then winds through Hudson Gardens and Event Center, a pastoral park that includes show gardens, ponds, walking trails, a miniature model train and a concert stage. (There is a 5k/10k run in the park every spring.) After another 0.5 mile, the trail enters South Platte Park, a large parcel of grasslands and wetlands buffering the river the remaining 3.0 miles to Chatfield State Park (see the "Other Denver Metro Routes" section later in this chapter). The trail crosses the C-470 Bikeway (Columbine Memorial Trail), ducks under the highway and enters the Chatfield trail system.

Alternate Routes: Heading northeast from Confluence Park, the route continues as the Platte River Greenway to Brighton, about 18 miles away. The trail system also connects to the C-470 Bikeway (Columbine Memorial Trail), Cherry Creek Bikeway (see page 23) and Sand Creek Regional Greenway (see page 40), making numerous long runs possible.

Wildlife: Deer, squirrels, raccoons, foxes and a variety of birds.
Weather: The route is easily accessed all year, although it can be icy in winter.
   The southern portion of the trail is more prone to wind than the north end.
Other Users: Cyclists, walkers and inline skaters.
Map: South Platte River District Map, City and County Denver, Department of
   Parks and Recreation.
Contact Info: (303) 937-4639, www.denvergov.org/south_platte_river.

Platte River Trail `Run 8`

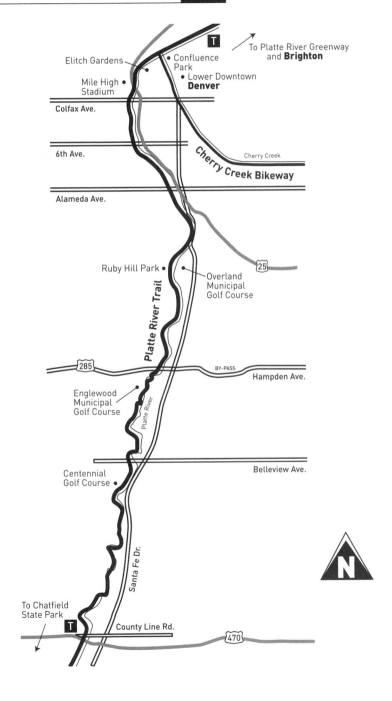

To Platte River Greenway
and **Brighton**

Elitch Gardens

Confluence
Park

Lower Downtown
Denver

Mile High
Stadium

Colfax Ave.

6th Ave.

Cherry Creek

Cherry Creek Bikeway

Alameda Ave.

Ruby Hill Park

Overland
Municipal
Golf Course

25

Platte River Trail

285

BY-PASS

Hampden Ave.

Englewood
Municipal
Golf Course

Platte River

Belleview Ave.

Centennial
Golf Course

Santa Fe Dr.

N

To Chatfield
State Park

County Line Rd.

470

Sand Creek Regional Greenway
(Aurora/Denver/Commerce City)
Run 9

Distance/Terrain: 13 miles (one way) on wide dirt and gravel trails and concrete bike paths.

Difficulty: Easy.

Elevation Change: Minimal. The trail has only a few minor hills.

Trailheads: Although it can be accessed in an unlimited number of places, there are four primary trailheads to Sand Creek Regional Greenway: near Smith Road and Laredo Street in Aurora (at Star K Ranch Open Space Area); Bluff Lake Nature Center between Peoria and Havana streets in east Denver; on Smith Road about 1 mile west of Havana Street in Denver; and near 56th Avenue and Dahlia (adjacent to I-270) in Commerce City.

Dogs: Yes, but they must be leashed at all times. Dogs are not allowed at Bluff Lake Nature Center.

Running Strollers: Yes, the smooth surfaces of the Sand Creek trail system are perfect for all types of running strollers.

Route Description: The Sand Creek Regional Greenway was completed in 2002 after six years of public and private entities working together. It meanders from Aurora through the Stapleton Redevelopment Site, under 1-70 and along I-270 until it ties into the northern section of the Platte Valley Greenway. Dubbed "Wilderness in the City" at its opening, it offers surprisingly wild surroundings in the heart of the most industrial sections of the Denver metro area. Because the terrain is flat and smooth and has very few road crossings, it's a great place to run uninterrupted workouts.

Starting from the eastern end of the route near Colfax Avenue just east of Airport Road, the Sand Creek trail weaves its way through residential Aurora in a northwesterly direction. Although there is no official trailhead at that end of the trail, there is usually parking available adjacent to the Roper Apparel and Footwear Distribution Center just east of the intersection of Sedalia Street and Colfax Avenue. The first trailhead connects with the trail about 1.5 miles to the northwest in Aurora's Star K Ranch Open Space area.

After crossing under Chambers Road (mile 2.0), the trail continues due west for about 2.0 miles as it passes under I-225 and meanders adjacent to Sand Creek Park and several residential areas. After it crosses under Peoria Street and into Denver's city limits, it leaves suburbia behind and enters one of the more wild

Sand Creek Regional Greenway   Run 9

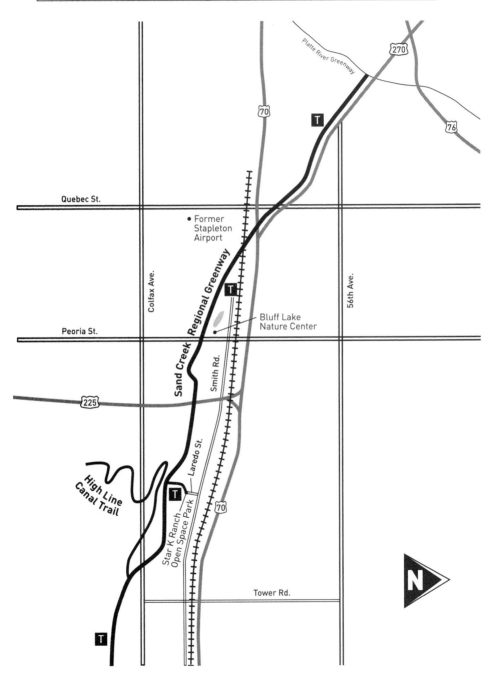

The new Sand Creek Regional Greenway (Run 9) stretches 13 miles through Aurora, Denver and Commerce City.

sections of the trail. The trail leaves the creek for about 1.0 mile as it ventures through the grassy fields and wetlands of Bluff Lake Nature Center—a fascinating 123-acre nature preserve at 3401 Quebec Street, Denver, that is probably the best place to start and end an out-and-back run.

The trail ducks under Havana Street (mile 5.75) and onto the former site of Stapleton International Airport. A portion of the land formerly used by the airport will be redeveloped as a 12,000-acre park with a major trailhead and additional Sand Creek feeder trails. Continuing in a northwesterly direction, the Sand Creek trail passes beneath two massive bridges that jumbo jets used while taxiing to and from the old runways north of I-70. You'll encounter an eerie tunnel-like darkness while running under these two bridges; the first is about 200 yards long, and the second is about 100 yards long.

When the trail pops out into daylight again, it crosses under a Union Pacific Railroad track (mile 6.5) near the midpoint of the Sand Creek Greenway system. From there, the trail passes near a warehouse district and then ducks under I-70 and Quebec Street as it enters Commerce City.

The remaining 5 or so miles along I-270 primarily consist of concrete bike paths and are distinctively less attractive than the previous sections. However, the

This section of Sand Creek Regional Greenway passes under the runway platforms of old Stapleton International Airport.

Sand Creek drainage basin is surprisingly full of foliage and wildlife, and new trees were planted in 2002 to spruce up a few sections. The only undesirable section of the Sand Creek trail system is the final 2.0 miles that runs adjacent to oil refineries and wastewater reclamation plants. You can continue to the northern section of the Platte Valley Greenway, but only if you can bear the stinky smell.

Alternate Routes: Believe it or not, but the Sand Creek Greenway completed a 50-mile off-road loop around the heart of Denver incorporating three other trails found in this book: Platte Valley Greenway, Cherry Creek Bikeway and Highline Canal Trail Northeast.

Wildlife: Deer, foxes, skunks, coyotes, raccoons and a variety of birds and raptors.
Weather: The trail is runnable year-round and typically has no icy or muddy sections.
Other Users: Cyclists, mountain bikers, walkers and horseback riders.
Map: Sand Creek Regional Greenway Map, 2002.
Contact Info: Sand Creek Regional Greenway, (303) 393-7700, www.sandcreek-greenway.org.

Washington Park (Denver)
Run 10

Distance/Terrain: 2.6 miles around the outer crushed-gravel loop, 1.6 miles around interior paved roads.

Difficulty: Easy.

Elevation Change: Minimal, unless you're stepping out of an oversized SUV.

Trailheads: This Denver park is located between Downing and Franklin streets and Virginia and Louisiana avenues, with entrances and parking available off Downing, Virginia and Franklin.

Dogs: Yes, but Boomer and Bart must be on a leash at all times.

Running Strollers: Yes, both the outer gravel loop and the interior roadways are suitable for running strollers. Keep your eyes peeled for cars and bikes on the interior loop and at park entrances.

Route Description: Wash Park, as it is called by anyone who has been there more than once, is an idyllic running retreat in the heart of south-central Denver. The crushed-gravel trail around the park's perimeter is one of the most frequented urban running trails on the Front Range. Even though it can get very crowded on weekends and weekday mornings, it's still a good place to get in a short run that will be mostly uninterrupted by traffic.

The loop is straightforward and flat but plenty scenic, with a variety of shade-bearing trees, grassy fields, flower gardens and three small ponds known as Smith Lake, Grasmere Lake and the Youth Fishing Pond. Soccer fields, volleyball and basketball courts, playgrounds and picnic areas dot the inside of the loop, as do several buildings—including a recreation center.

If running loops on the 2.6-mile outer circuit gets monotonous, there are plenty of ways to mix things up with the inner paved loop and the 1.0-mile circle between the two largest ponds. "I've run between 5 and 15 miles there and have never done the same route twice," says Denver marathoner Steve Betz. "You've got to make the most of what you have there, otherwise you'll get bored in a hurry."

There are numerous 5k and 10k races held in Wash Park every year, including the Mile High United Way Turkey Trot 4-miler and the 5k Jingle Bell Run. Visit www.bkbltd.com for details.

Wildlife: Ducks, geese, squirrels, rabbits and raccoons.

Weather: Denver is one of the sunniest cities in the U.S., and Wash Park always seems to be drenched in sunlight.

Washington Park Run 10

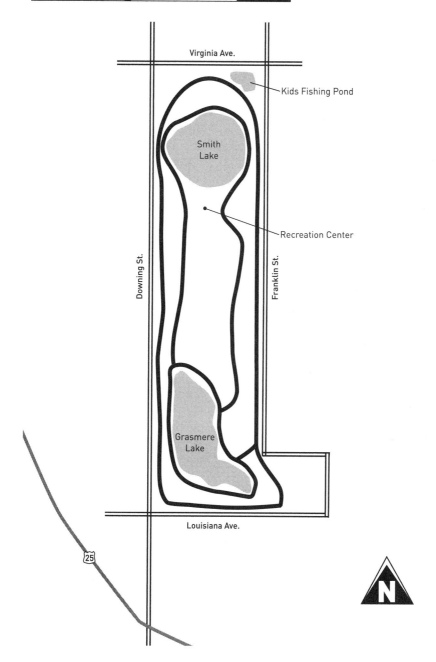

Virginia Ave.

Kids Fishing Pond

Smith Lake

Recreation Center

Downing St.

Franklin St.

Grasmere Lake

Louisiana Ave.

25

N

Rachel Price does an early morning tempo run around Smith Lake at
Denver's Washington Park.

Other Users: Walkers, inline skaters and cyclists. Bikes and skates are prohibited
on the gravel running path, but jogging strollers are allowed.

Map: Washington Park Map, City and County of Denver, Department of Parks
and Recreation.

Contact Info: (303)964-2580, www.denvergov.org.

Other Denver Metro Routes

1. Cherry Creek State Park, Aurora
Distance: 8.0 miles. Difficulty: Easy. An 8.0-mile loop of paved and fine-gravel trails begins and ends at the west entrance of the park near the intersection of Union Avenue and Dayton Street. The top portion of the loop parallels the road to the east entrance and passes a campground on the north side of the reservoir. The trail then follows the eastern perimeter of the park all the way down to Twelve Mile Area (a marshy area in the southeast corner of the park) along the meandering banks of the Cherry Creek. The loop crosses the creek several times and continues in a northwesterly direction back to the west entrance. A $6 admission fee is required to enter the park. For information, call (303) 690-1166, or go to www.parks.state.co.us.

2. Chatfield State Park, Littleton
Distance: 4 to 20 miles. Difficulty: Easy. This expansive park on the southeast side of the Denver metro area has numerous loops to run without ever having to repeat the same section twice. A good place to start is near the horse corrals south of the Wadsworth Boulevard entrance. The trail begins as a long dirt fire road that parallels Wadsworth about 2.5 miles to the southwest corner of the park, dropping slightly in elevation along the way. The trail cuts to the east for a bit, then curls back to the north in a wooded singletrack section along the South Platte River. Just before the road bridge over the river, follow the trail to the left and head back to the horse corrals to complete a 6.0-mile loop or cross the bridge and add more mileage on trails east of Chatfield Reservoir. Ultrarunning guru Scott Weber typically hosts several trail races (www.coachweber.com) at the park every year. (He moved to South Carolina in 2003 but planned on continuing his race series.) A $6 admission fee is required to enter the park, unless you're running in a race. For information, call (303) 791-7275, or go to www.parks.state.co.us.

3. Clear Creek Bikeway, Golden/Commerce City
Distance: Up to 14 miles (one way). Difficulty: Easy to moderate. The Clear Creek Bikeway runs from the east side of Golden to Commerce City via the Wheatridge Greenbelt with only one minor interruption. It's a wide concrete bike path with few road crossings and very little change in elevation. Although it is popular with cyclists, it is never crowded. For information, call (303) 235-2877, or go to www.ci.wheatridge.co.us/parks.html.

Creigh Kelley: Denver's Running Man

C reigh Kelley gets up just about every morning at 5:15, pulls on his running shoes and heads out for his daily run with a couple of neighbors. Sometimes he ventures over to Highline Canal Trail; other mornings he just runs the roads in Denver's south suburbs near his home.

"I just love running," says Kelley, a former 2:32 marathoner and sub-32-minute 10k runner. "I very rarely jump into a race, but I'll never stop running."

For nearly 25 years, Kelley has been tied to the running community along Colorado's Front Range. First he was one of the top running-shoe retailers in Denver, operating six Phidippides running stores from the late 1970s to the late 1980s. He also helped start Denver's Phidippides Track Club, one of the oldest and continuously active recreational running clubs in Colorado.

In 1980, during the peak of America's initial running boom, Kelley and his friends Ken Buckius and Doug Busch had a vision—to start a company that would organize and time running races. It doesn't sound like that much of a brainstorm now, but back then most races were organized by volunteers and running clubs. With $50, they started BKB Ltd. and hit the ground running with a few small races.

"We thought it would be fun to put on races, but we didn't know what we were doing," says Kelley, who turned 56 in 2002. "It was very, very controversial. I had people screaming at me, telling me I was ruining their sport because I was doing it as a business. It was somewhat shocking."

BKB remained a fledgling company through the late 1980s, but then started to boom when the population of the Front Range began to swell. In 2003, BKB is by far the largest race-production company in Colorado and one of the biggest in the North America, organizing more than 50 running races, triathlons and cycling events in Colorado, Texas, Washington and Mexico.

A few of BKB's most popular events include the Runnin' of the Green Lucky 7k in Denver's Lower Downtown in March, the Georgetown to Idaho Springs Half Marathon in August and the Mile High United Way Turkey Trot 4-miler in Denver's Washington Park on Thanksgiving Day.

Still, Kelley's reach goes far beyond race directing. A Vietnam War veteran and father of three, he has coached various U.S. running teams in international competitions, served as an agent for a handful of world-class athletes and held positions with USA Track & Field, the national governing body of competitive running in the U.S. He's also been an

Denver's Creigh Kelley has been a race promoter, agent, announcer and accomplished runner.

emcee, announcer and award-winning commentator at numerous races around the world.

Plus, the vast majority of BKB's races benefit local or national non-profit organizations, including the Rape Assistance and Awareness Program, Denver's St. Joseph Hospital Foundation, the Prostate Cancer Education Council and the Children's Miracle Network.

"I picked his brain as much as I could when I started our race," says Beth Luther, race director for the Slacker Half Marathon and 5k from Loveland ski area to Georgetown. "I took his words as gold. He's been doing this for a long time, and he really knows the industry well."

Denver Metro Running Resources

Track Facilities

The Denver metro area has several good all-weather tracks ideal for speed workouts. Here are a few of the better ones:

* All City Stadium/Denver South High School, 1700 E. Louisiana Ave., Denver
* Broomfield High School, 1000 W. Daphne St., Broomfield
* Centaurus High School, 10300 South Boulder Rd., Lafayette
* Cherry Creek High School, 9300 East Union Ave., Greenwood Village
* Columbine High School, 6201 S. Pierce St., Littleton
* Five Star Stadium, Washington St. and Eppinger Blvd., Thornton
* Highlands Ranch High School, 9375 South Cresthill Lane., Highlands Ranch
* JeffCo Stadium, 540 Kipling Ave., Lakewood
* Thomas Jefferson High School, 3950 S. Holly St., Denver

Group Runs

Colorado Columbines

is a women's running club that meets for monthly runs, weekly track workouts
and more. Call (303) 332-9858 or visit www.angelfire.com/co/coloradocolumbines
for more details.

Denver Track Club

holds several community track meets each summer at Rangeview High School in
Aurora (17599 E. Iliff Ave.). The meets begin at 8:30 A.M. Visit www.denvertrack-
club.org for more details.

Denver Trail Runners

meets on Wednesday mornings and Thursday evenings for group trail runs, usually
in the Morrison/Golden area, and occasionally on weekends for longer runs. Visit
http://groups.yahoo.com/group/DenverTrailRunners for more details.

Niketown Running Club

holds runs of 3, 5 and 7 miles every Tuesday at 5:30 P.M. at the Niketown Denver
store in the Denver Pavilions shopping area near 16th Street and Glenarm Place in
downtown Denver. Call (303) 623-6453 for more details.

Phidippides Track Club

meets for interval workouts on the track at Belleview Elementary School in Englewood (4851 S. Dayton St.) every Tuesday from March through October. Visit www.phidippides.org for more details.

Rocky Mountain Road Runners

meets several times each week: Tuesday evenings at Washington Park in Denver; Wednesday evenings for track workouts at Denver South High School (1700 E. Louisiana Ave.); Saturday mornings for a variety of runs around the metro area; and Sunday mornings at Waterton Canyon State Park. Visit www.rmrr.org for more details.

Running Retailers

Boulder Running Company

8116 W. Bowles Ave., Unit C, Littleton

(303) 932-6000

www.boulderrunningcompany.com

Eastern Mountain Sports

870 S. Colorado Blvd., Suite D, Glendale

(303) 759-3080

www.ems.com

Eastern Mountain Sports—Park Meadows Mall

8405 Park Meadows Center Dr., Suite 1006, Littleton

(303) 790-0760

www.ems.com

Galyan's—Flatirons Crossing Mall

31 West Flatiron Circle, Broomfield

(720) 887-0900

Galyan's—Park Meadows Mall

8435 Park Meadows Center Dr., Littleton

(720) 479-0600

Several races run through the heart of LoDo, including the Runnin' of the Green Lucky 7k in mid-March.

Niketown Denver—Denver Pavilions
500 16th St., Denver
(303) 623-6453
www.niketown.com

REI (flagship store)
1416 Platte St., Denver
(303) 756-3100
www.rei.com

REI
9637 E. County Line Rd., Englewood
(303) 858-1726
www.rei.com

REI
5375 S. Wadsworth Blvd., Lakewood
(303) 932-0600
www.rei.com

Runners Roost

6554 S. Parker Rd., Aurora

(303) 766-3411

www.runnersroost.com

Runners Roost

1979 E. County Line Rd., Highlands Ranch

(303) 738-9446

www.runnersroost.com

Runners Roost

1685 S. Colorado Blvd., Denver

(303) 759-8455

www.runnersroost.com

The Sporting Woman

2902 E. Third Ave., Denver

(303) 316-8392

www.thesportingwoman.com

Two Feet to Go

3875 Tennyson St., Denver

(303) 458-7700

Beth Reece and Jason Smith charge up Anemone Trail in Boulder.

Boulder

Boulder is known as one of the world's top running meccas—and with good reason. Dozens of world-class road, track and ultradistance runners and triathletes—from both the U.S. and countries from around the globe—train in Boulder. Still, it's the regular citizens and the diverse topography that really set Boulder apart. Not only does a large percentage of the population run, the city boasts more than 180 miles of close-in trails and one of the world's top road races, the Bolder Boulder 10k.

Every day of the year you can find dedicated Boulderites hoofing it up the steep trails in the foothills, cruising the routes near Boulder Reservoir or doing interval workouts on one of the tracks around town. The "People's Republic of Boulder" gets plenty of abuse from outsiders who believe the city's eclectic population thinks there is no place in the world that compares. But as a running community, there truly is no place in the world quite like Boulder.

Boulder Creek Path Run 11

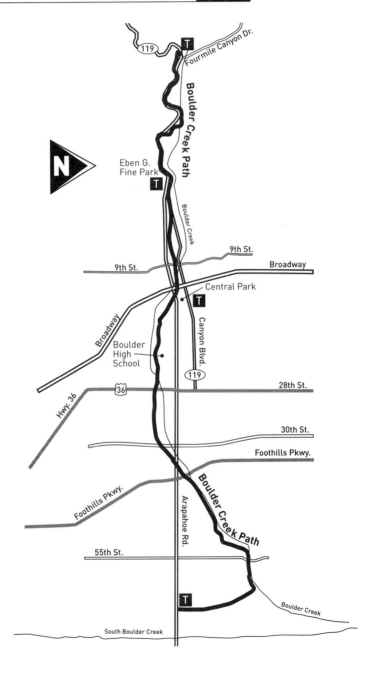

Boulder Creek Path
Run 11

Distance/Terrain: Up to 7.2 miles (one way) on a wide concrete bicycle path and adjacent dirt paths (in the city), and a wide dirt and gravel trail (in Boulder Canyon).

Difficulty: Easy.

Elevation Change: Minimal.

Trailheads: Eben G. Fine Park. There are also numerous other access points throughout the city, including the Boulder Public Library, University of Colorado, the Millennium Hotel, Scott Carpenter Park, Potts Field and Stazio Ballfields in east Boulder. Public restroom facilities are located at Eben G. Fine Park and at the library.

Dogs: Dogs are allowed on Boulder Creek Path but must be on a leash at all times.

Jogging Strollers: Yes, the flat and smooth surfaces of the path are ideal for jogging strollers.

Route Description: If you don't mind running on concrete, the Boulder Creek Path can be a great route for short to medium-length runs. But it's an even better place for people watching. The path has two distinct sections: a flat 5.0-mile concrete path that follows Boulder Creek from Eben G. Fine Park to the east side of town; and a 2.2-mile section that turns to a wide dirt and gravel travel trail as it winds gradually up into Boulder Canyon. Most of the concrete sections are complemented by parallel dirt paths or grassy sections.

In the summer and on mild weekends throughout the year, the path can be packed with walkers, bicyclists, runners and tourists, so it's best to run it early in the morning. If you run it at off-peak times, the creek path offers a peaceful escape along gently bubbling Boulder Creek—especially because it is completely devoid of road crossings.

East from Eben G. Fine Park: Starting from the 0.0 mileage marker near the east bridge in Eben G. Fine Park, the path winds through the heart of downtown Boulder on the north side of the creek. In the first mile, you run past the city's Justice Center, where a grand jury failed to indict John and Patsy Ramsey in the JonBenet Ramsey murder case in the late 1990s. (Immediately after leaving the park, the path intersects with a 0.5-mile singletrack trail that is off-limits to bikes. It's an idyllic soft-surface escape in during the day, but it's probably not a wise place to run alone at dusk or after dark.)

From hippies to yuppies to world-class athletes, Boulder Creek Path sees all kinds.

The path crosses under 9th Street and approaches the Boulder Public Library, a two-building structure that straddles the creek and is connected by a walkway overpass. After passing by the library lawns (mile 1.0) and City Hall, the creek dips under Broadway and pops up in Central Park—home to hippies, the homeless and a historic narrow-gauge train that throttled up Boulder Canyon in the early 1900s. From there, the trail ducks under Arapahoe Avenue and parallels Boulder High School's athletic fields in a long straightaway, skirts through the lower section of the University of Colorado (mile 2.0) and past the Millennium Hotel, where the trail crosses back to the south side of the creek. From there, it ducks under 28th Street, behind an apartment complex and along the south edge of Scott Carpenter Park. The path continues under 30th Street, past the north side of Potts Field and CU's track-and-field complex and eventually under Arapahoe Avenue (mile 3.0) for a second time.

When the trail pops up on the east side of Foothills Parkway, you'll cross another bridge and again be running on the north side of the creek behind a large office complex. The path passes under a railroad track, veers away from the creek and joins a sidewalk adjacent to Pearl Parkway (mile 4.0). Go right and continue following the path to the east past a series of ponds. The path drops under 55th Street and behind another office complex, where Boulder Creek spills into a holding reservoir. As the trail curves to the south (mile 5.0), it begins following South Boulder Creek upstream and passes an offshoot that leads to Stazio Ballfields. Boulder Creek Path officially ends on Arapahoe Avenue near an intersection with Cherryvale Road, about 5 miles from Eben G. Fine Park.

West from Eben G. Fine Park: From Eben G. Fine Park, run the Creek Path west into Boulder Canyon adjacent to Highway 119 (Canyon Boulevard) and Boulder Creek. The first mile (on a concrete path) climbs gradually to a popular picnic and rock climbing area, so don't be surprised if you're huffing and puffing a bit. Keep your eyes peeled for rock climbers high on the canyon walls, 100-year-old stone bridge abutments of the Colorado & Northwestern Railway and fast-paced mountain bikers on their way back to Boulder.

Near mile 1.0, the trail turns to soft gravel, crosses the creek on a bridge and meanders at a gradual incline along the north side of the creek for about a mile before crossing back to the south side of the creek. The trail ducks under the road and ends about 400 yards later at a small parking area west of the intersection of Highway 119 and Fourmile Canyon Drive.

Alternate Route: There are several other trails accessible from Eben G. Fine Park, including routes to Red Rocks/Anemone Trail, Sunshine Canyon and Mount Sanitas to the north and Flagstaff Mountain (via Viewpoint Trail) to the south.

Wildlife: Ducks, foxes, skunks, geese, deer, rainbow trout, a wide variety of birds
Weather: There are plenty of viaducts and shelters to hide under in case it rains.
The path is well maintained in winter and is often plowed (to a point just west of Eben G. Fine Park) before the city's roads.
Other Users: Cyclists, walkers, stroller pushers and jugglers.
Map: City of Boulder Open Space & Mountain Parks, 2002.
Contact Info: (303) 441-3440, www.ci.boulder.co.us/openspace.

East Boulder Trail
Teller Farms/White Rocks
Run 12

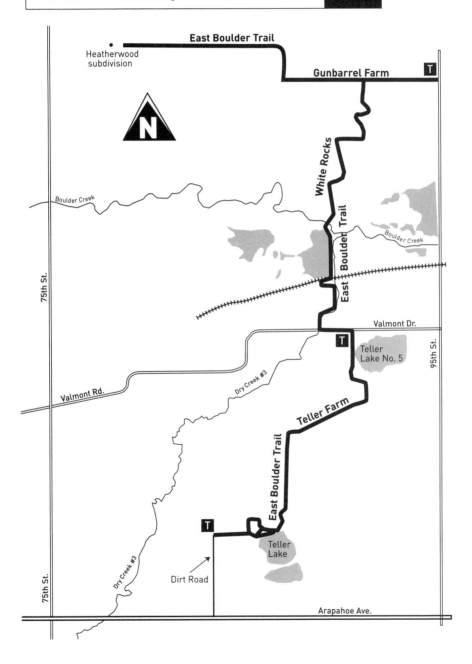

East Boulder Trail
Teller Farms/White Rocks
Run 12

Distance/Terrain: 10.0 miles (round-trip) on wide gravel trails and singletrack dirt trails.

Difficulty: Easy to moderate.

Elevation Change: Minimal, except for one steep climb and a series of rolling hills on the north end.

Trailheads: East Boulder Trail's Teller Farm South trailhead on Arapahoe Avenue, 1.25 miles east of 75th Street. Restroom facilities are available at the trailhead. Another trailhead is located on Valmont Road about 1.5 miles east of 75th.

Dogs: Dogs are allowed on the Teller Farm portion of the trail (south of Valmont Road) but must be under voice and sight control. Dogs are prohibited on the White Rocks section of the trail north of Valmont Road because of the wildlife preserve.

Jogging Strollers: Yes, jogging strollers work well on the southern portion of the trail, but it can get a bit too bumpy and rutted after the railroad crossing in the northern section.

Route Description: East Boulder Trail is really two trails combined to make a longer one. The south section of the route (between Arapahoe and Valmont) runs through lush Teller Farm, where ranchers have grazed cattle for more than 100 years. The north section (north of Valmont) includes the lush terrain in the Boulder Creek Valley, as well as the especially arid terrain above the White Rocks plateau. Both sides offer extraordinary views of the Front Range mountains, including Boulder's Bear Peak and Green Mountain to the south and massive Longs Peak to the north.

From the Teller Farm South trailhead, the trail runs due east for about 0.5 mile, curves around Teller Lake and heads due north along fields of native grasses and lilac bushes. After 1.4 miles, the trail turns right and heads northeast along a drainage ditch shrouded occasionally by large old willows and poplars. From there, the trail crosses an old wooden wagon bridge and meanders past a series of small oil wells to another trailhead at Valmont Road (mile 2.7)

Follow the trail out of the northwest corner of the trailhead's parking lot for 200 yards and cross Valmont Road—*be careful to watch for cars!*—to pick up the start of the White Rocks portion of East Boulder Trail. (Remember, no dogs allowed!) The trail meanders northward along Dry Creek #3 and crosses the original

Lisa Jhung and her dog, Hanna, are out for a leisurely run on East Boulder Trail.

railroad line into Boulder—a now-defunct Union Pacific line that dates back to 1872. After crossing the tracks (which are slated for removal in 2003), you'll pass a series of ponds (formerly gravel pits) that serve as a protected wildlife sanctuary for more than 150 species of birds, fish and mammals.

The route continues northward, crosses Boulder Creek on a 50-foot wood-and-steel bridge (mile 3.8) and then ventures up the dry and dusty ridge of the White Rocks Plateau. (Look to the west to see amazing white sandstone cliffs, but stay away, because they're located on private property.) After climbing a short, steep hill, the trail rolls up and down a series of hills before intersecting with Gunbarrel Farm Trail (mile 5.0). Turn around and head back the same way for one of the best rural runs in Boulder.

Alternate Routes: To tack on a few more miles, run west on Gunbarrel Farm Trail for 1.7 miles to the Heatherwood subdivision before heading back to East Boulder Trail and the Teller Farm South trailhead. That total round-trip is about 13.5 miles. You also can lengthen your round-trip by an additional mile by heading east at the intersection of Gunbarrel Farm and East Boulder trails, and following the Gunbarrel Farm Trail for 0.5 mile to the trailhead on 95th Street.

Wildlife: Deer, skunks, foxes, coyotes, snakes, falcons, hawks, eagles and raccoons.
Weather: East Boulder Trail offers very little shade or shelter, so running on a windy or hot day can be brutal. The trail is very runnable in winter months, but a portion of the trail north of Valmont often floods in the spring when Dry Creek #3 overflows its banks.
Other Users: Mountain bikers, hikers and stroller pushers.
Map: City of Boulder Open Space & Mountain Parks, 2002.
Contact Info: (303) 441-3440, www.ci.boulder.co.us/openspace.

Flagstaff Mountain
Run 13

Distance/Terrain: 5.0 miles (round-trip) on steep singletrack dirt trails.
Difficulty: Hard.
Elevation Change: Moderate. The trail climbs about 1,300 feet from the Chautauqua parking area to the 6,870-foot summit of Flagstaff Mountain.
Trailheads: You can park at Gregory Canyon, near the junction of Flagstaff and Baseline roads in Boulder, but it's smarter to park at Chautauqua Park

Flagstaff Mountain Run 13

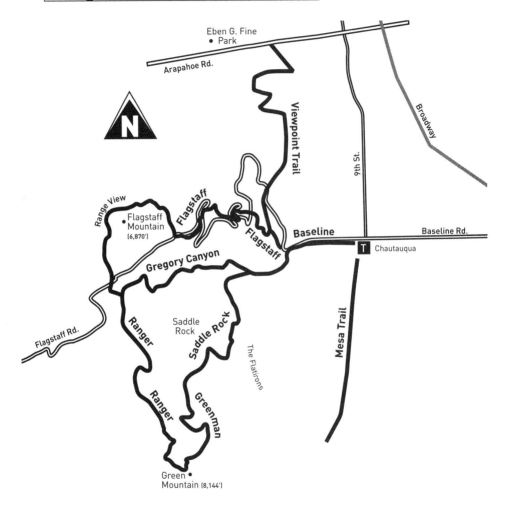

near 9th Street and Baseline. Not only is it easier to find a parking spot, but you'll be glad you had the extra 0.5 mile to warm up before starting the grueling climb.

Dogs: Dogs are allowed but must be under voice and sight control. This route crosses busy roads seven times, so be careful not to let dogs dart ahead too far.

Jogging Strollers: No, definitely not.

Route Description: This can be an arduous run if you're not used to running hills, but you'll be rewarded with spectacular views of Boulder and the thrill of reaching the summit of Flagstaff Mountain. It's only a 5.0-mile loop from the Chautauqua Park trailhead, but the climbing can make it feel like 10. There are numerous places to stop and enjoy the views, so take advantage of them if you need to catch your breath. The entire loop will take between 40 and 75 minutes, depending on your pace.

Start the run by heading east from the entrance to Chautauqua Park on Baseline Trail. After about 0.5 mile, take the fork in the trail that drops down to Baseline Road. Flagstaff Trail begins with a few stair steps in the tall grasses just across the road that leads to the Gregory Canyon parking area. Flagstaff Trail climbs about 300 feet in the first 0.5 mile, including a few super-steep sections that will slow most people to a walk. But after passing the junction with View Point Trail, the route becomes much less steep for the next 0.5 mile—which gives you a much-needed chance to catch your breath and return to a normal running stride. But that rest is short-lived because, after the fifth road crossing (mile 1.75), the trail steepens on the way to the summit.

You know you're near the top when you cross a paved park road. Continue across that road to the right of the stone wall and follow the trail to the intersection with Ute Trail (mile 2.2). From there, look for Range View Trail and follow it to the west as it winds through the trees and around the back side of Flagstaff Mountain. Along the way, keep your eyes peeled for stunning views of the high mountains of the Indian Peaks Wilderness Area along the Continental Divide.

When the trail pops out at a parking lot on Flagstaff Road (mile 2.8), cross the road, run around the closed vehicle gate and go down a wide trail about 500 yards. Curl around the Gregory Canyon trailhead sign on your left and get ready for an exhilarating downhill. After about 0.5 mile of up-and-down terrain, the rugged, rock-strewn Gregory Canyon Trail drops about 1,000 feet in 1.4 miles. Watch your footing! When you get to the parking lot at the bottom, cross the wooden bridge next to the trailhead signs and then veer left to find Baseline Trail (mile 4.5). If you have any energy, jog the final 0.5 mile back to the Chautauqua parking knowing you just ran one of Boulder's signature mountains.

Alternate Routes: If you've already run Flagstaff, you might as well run the 6.5-mile loop to the top of 8,144-foot Green Mountain and back. It's considerably harder, but much more rewarding. From Chautauqua Park, run east on Baseline Trail for 0.5 miles and then up Gregory Canyon Trail. At mile 2.0, take a left on Ranger Trail and run its 1.3 leg-burning, lung-busting miles to an intersection with West Ridge Trail. Run the West Ridge Trail the final 0.2 miles to the summit and enjoy one of the best views in Boulder. Take E.M. Greenman Trail down the front side, veer right on Saddle Rock Trail and complete the 2.8-mile descent back to Chautauqua.

Wildlife: Deer, foxes, raccoons, skunks, mountain lions, bears. (Mountain lions and bears are often spotted on these trails, so know what to do if you encounter one. See page 12 of "Wildlife.")

Weather: This loop can be run year-round, although both Flagstaff and Gregory Canyon trails can be icy in winter and very muddy in spring.

Other Users: Hikers and tourists; mountain bikers are not allowed on any of these trails.

Map: City of Boulder Open Space & Mountain Parks, 2002.

Contact Info: (303) 441-3440, www.ci.boulder.co.us/openspace.

Heil Valley Ranch
Wapiti–Ponderosa Loop
Run 14

Distance/Terrain: 7.8 miles (round-trip) on a technical singletrack dirt trail.

Difficulty: Moderate.

Elevation Change: Moderate. The trail climbs about 1,000 feet from the trailhead to the high point of the loop.

Trailhead: Located on Geer Canyon Drive, about a 10-minute drive north of Boulder. Take Highway 36 north and go left on Lefthand Canyon Drive. Geer Canyon Drive and a Heil Valley Ranch sign can be seen on the north side of the road about a 0.8 miles west of Highway 36. Go north about 1 mile on Geer Canyon Drive to reach the trailhead.

Dogs: Leave Fido at home; dogs are not allowed, and rangers have been known to write $50 tickets without warnings.

Jogging Strollers: No, definitely not.

Heil Valley Ranch Wapiti-Ponderosa Loop

Run 14

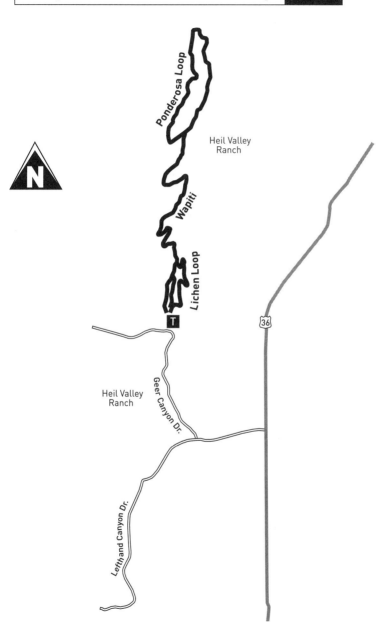

Route Description: Completed in 2001, the Wapiti–Ponderosa Loop is one of the newest running trails in the Boulder Open Space & Mountain Parks system. Because it's one of the few technical mountain bike trails close to Boulder, it's often packed with fat-tire enthusiasts, some of which like to really bomb it on the way back down to the parking lot. It's one of the best trail runs near Boulder, but it's wise to run defensively or you might wind up eating tire treads. The entire loop will take 1.25 to 1.45 hours, depending on your pace.

Wapiti Trail begins as a dirt road that heads north out of the main parking area. After 0.5 mile, the route turns into a singletrack trail, veers to the left and begins the 2.1-mile winding ascent to Ponderosa Loop. The trail is generally clear of loose rocks, but there are plenty of roots, gullies and other obstacles. The route gets steeper as it goes, so expect to be breathing heartily when you finally reach Ponderosa Loop.

The 2.6-mile loop has two very gradual climbs, but it has plenty of technical features, so it's difficult to run fast. The loop concludes back at the junction of Wapiti Trail, so unless you're going to do multiple laps (which is a good way to boost your mileage on this trail), make the turn and head back to the parking lot. It's easy to run fast on the 2.7-mile descent, but keep your eyes peeled for obstacles and other trail users.

Alternate Routes: The only adjacent trail in the Heil Valley Ranch Open Space is Lichen Loop Trail, which only adds another 0.8 mile. The trail begins and ends near the wooden bridge at the northeast corner of the parking lot. A smarter and more fun way to add 2.6 miles is to run a second lap, in the opposite direction to the first, on the Ponderosa Loop.

Wildlife: Deer, foxes, coyotes, bobcats, mountain lions, possums, bears, raccoons and prairie dogs.
Weather: The trail is accessible year-round, but don't be fooled by sunny skies and a clear trail when you start. Because it is buried in the trees at a higher elevation, the Ponderosa Loop can hold snow and ice much longer than the lower Wapiti Trail, and it's often a little cooler up top than it is in the parking lot.
Other Users: Mountain bikers, hikers and horseback riders.
Map: City of Boulder Open Space & Mountain Parks, 2002.
Contact Info: (303) 441-3440, www.ci.boulder.co.us/openspace.

Marshall Mesa Loop
Run 15

Distance/Terrain: 6.5 miles (round-trip) on variety of dirt and gravel trails.

Difficulty: Easy to moderate.

Elevation Change: Moderate. There are only three medium-size hills on
the entire loop.

Trailheads: Flatirons Vista trailhead on Highway 93, about 1.5 miles south of the
Eldorado Springs Drive–Marshall Drive intersection. You can also access this
loop from the Doudy Draw trailhead on Eldorado Springs Drive, about 1.5 miles
west of Highway 93 or the Marshall Mesa trailhead on Marshall Drive about
1 mile east of Highway 93.

Dogs: Yes, but dogs must be under sight and voice control, especially near livestock
grazing in open space. (Also, be careful with dogs while crossing Highway 93.)

Jogging Strollers: Not recommended. The big hill west of the Flatirons Vista trailhead is too steep and rugged, and the highway crossings are too dangerous.

Route Description: One of the better loop trail runs near Boulder, the Community
Ditch, Doudy Draw and Greenbelt Plateau circuit offers spectacular views of
Boulder's jagged mountains, Denver's skyline and Eldorado Canyon. It's typically
less crowded than other Boulder trails, but has a lot of equestrian traffic on weekends. The entire loop will take 50 to 90 minutes to complete, depending on your
pace and where you start.

From the Flatirons Vista trailhead, Doudy Draw Trail begins with a moderate
300-yard climb but flattens out as it heads due west for about 1.2 miles on a high
grassy plateau. Near the western edge of the plateau, the trail turns southward
and cuts through a pine grove that overlooks Eldorado Mountain. From there, the
trail begins dropping, turns 180 degrees and heads north and continues dropping
down to the creek basin in Doudy Draw. After going up a short slope of about 25
feet, the trail sneaks through a gate in a fence and begins a long, gradual downhill
to the intersection with Community Ditch Trail (mile 2.8).

From there, go right and run northeast for 1.7 flat miles along the meandering
Community Ditch. Go through the gate at Highway 93, look both ways and scurry
across the road. You'll see two trail gates within 25 yards—take the one to the
south, in front of you to the right of the steel guardrail. At that point, you're running on Greenbelt Plateau Trail, which curves up and over its namesake ridge
while heading southward toward Highway 128. When you get to the trailhead, jog
down to the intersection of Highway 128 and 93, cross over to the west side of

Marshall Mesa Loop `Run 15`

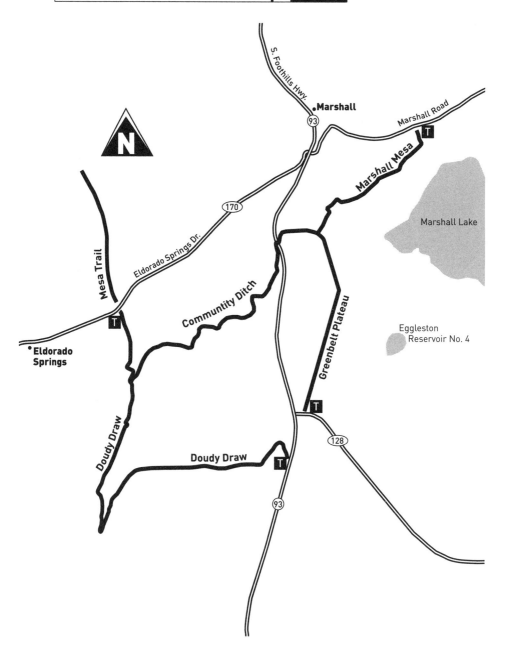

Highway 93—very carefully!—and run the shoulder 300 yards back to the Flatirons Vista trailhead.

Alternate Routes: Double the length of your run by running a second loop counter-clockwise. You can also add an additional 3 miles to this loop if you start from the Marshall Mesa trailhead. The 1.5-mile Marshall Mesa Trail connects to the loop at the north end of the Greenbelt Plateau section. The rich coal-mining history of the Marshall area is depicted in an interpretive sign tour along the Marshall Mesa Trail.

Wildlife: Deer, foxes, coyotes, skunks, squirrels, hawks, falcons and occasionally some antelope.

Weather: Virtually the entire trail is exposed, which can make running this route quite difficult if not downright ugly in hot or windy conditions. You can run the trail year-round, but sections of the loop are prone to deep snowdrifts in the winter months and very sticky mud in the spring.

Other Users: Hikers, horseback riders and mountain bikers. (Bikes are allowed only on the Community Ditch and Greenbelt Plateau sections).

Map: City of Boulder Open Space & Mountain Parks, 2002.

Contact Info: (303) 441-3440, www.ci.boulder.co.us/openspace.

Mesa Trail
Run 16

Distance/Terrain: 7 miles (one way) on rolling, technical singletrack trail.

Difficulty: Medium.

Elevation Change: Moderate, with a few strenuous uphills

Trailheads: Chautauqua Park, near 9th Street and Baseline Road in Boulder. A second trailhead is adjacent to Eldorado Springs Drive, about 1.5 miles west of Highway 93.

Dogs: Yes, but must be under voice and sight control at all times. Because of the danger of mountain lions, it's wise to keep your dog on leash, especially if you're running alone.

Jogging Strollers: Definitely not. The trail is too rugged.

Route Description: If all communities had trail systems like this one, no one would ever pound the pavement again. The consummate Front Range running route, Mesa

Mesa Trail Run 16

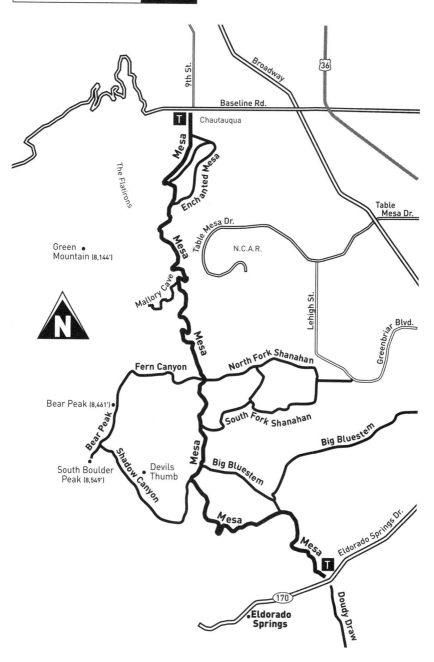

Trail is a rugged but very scenic trail just moments from downtown Boulder. It meanders its way south from Boulder's Chautauqua Park (near 9th and Baseline) to the south Mesa trailhead in the small community of Eldorado Springs, although there are many offshoots that make other loop runs possible. There are many out-and-back trail runs available from Chautauqua Park, but Mesa Trail is an ideal point-to-point run if you can drop a car or have someone pick you up at the southern trailhead.

Although quite crowded on weekends, Mesa Trail gets surprisingly little traffic during the week. Unlike some of the steeper trails in Boulder, Mesa Trail is accessible to runners of all abilities and takes between 50 and 90 minutes to complete from north to south.

From the trailhead at the Chautauqua ranger station, Mesa Trail begins as a roughly paved road that climbs 0.6 mile to the start of the singletrack dirt trail. This rock-strewn dirt trail zigzags and climbs for about 1.5 miles, then plateaus for about 1 mile as it hangs on a ledge below the Flatirons. After crossing a meadow, it drops down a series of steps into Skunk Canyon. Once at the bottom of the canyon, it rises to a meadow behind the National Center for Atmospheric Research (NCAR).

Once atop a small hill, the trail passes a fork to Mallory Cave (see below) and begins a 0.25-mile descent into Bear Canyon. The trail widens to a gravel road at the bottom of Bear Canyon and then begins a steep, winding 0.75-mile ascent to a high plateau and the midway point of the trail. The trail takes a sharp right off of the road and back onto technical singletrack, beginning a 1.2-mile stretch of spectacular rolling hills. After crossing another meadow, the trail tops out and begins the 1.75-mile, twisting fire road descent to Mesa trailhead and parking area on Eldorado Springs Drive.

Alternate Route: Instead of starting your run up the paved road, take Enchanted Mesa trail, which begins next to a picnic shelter behind the historic Chautauqua Auditorium. After crossing a creek via an old stone bridge, the trail climbs gradually for about 1.5 miles to a junction with Kohler Mesa Trail. Go left at the fork and follow Kohler Mesa Trail as it drops down off a high mesa onto a gravel road and then curves back southward toward Skunk Canyon. After running 2 miles on Kohler Mesa, you'll come to a junction. Make a right onto Skunk Canyon Trail and begin a rugged 1-mile climb to Mesa Trail. If you run back to the Chautauqua auditorium from there, you will have earned every bit of the 4.5-mile loop.

* If you're looking for a steeper adventure, take the Mallory Cave spur from the meadow behind NCAR. It climbs 0.6 miles up a very steep route that ends at a rock slab below the modest-size cave. The upper portion of the Mallory Cave Spur is closed on occasion during the spring and summer to protect the roosting of western (Townsend's) big-eared bats.

Wildlife: Deer, foxes, squirrels, coyotes, skunks, mountain lions and bears.

Be especially careful running alone at dusk when mountain lions are looking for their dinner.

Weather: Most of the Mesa Trail system is heavily shaded by large pine groves, so runners can often escape wind and summer heat and rain showers. The trail is runnable year-round, although it can be very slippery when ice and snow collect on north-facing slopes and extremely muddy during spring thaw.

Other Users: Hikers and horseback riders. Mountain bikers are not allowed on Mesa Trail or any of its adjoining trails.

Map: City of Boulder Open Space & Mountain Parks, 2002.

Contact Info: (303) 441-3440, www.ci.boulder.co.us/openspace.

Mount Sanitas and Dakota Ridge Trail
Run 17

Distance/Terrain: 3.5 miles (round-trip) on rocky singletrack trails.

Difficulty: Hard.

Elevation Change: Moderate to extreme. The route up Mount Sanitas is grueling— so grueling that it's only about 60 to 70 percent runnable for most runners. But it's an epic workout that will build strength for road and trail racing.

Trailhead: Park at the Mount Sanitas trailhead on Mapleton Avenue about three blocks west of 4th Street.

Dogs: Yes, dogs are allowed but must be under voice and sight control at all times.

Running Strollers: No way. The trail is too technical and steep.

Route Description: Only a select few mountain-running fiends can run this with any consistency. For everyone else, it's an absolute grind. Start at the shelter near the main parking area and begin the 1.4-mile ascent to Sanitas' 6,730-foot summit. Take a left at the first trail junction (about 50 feet into the run) and get ready to start gasping. The trail crosses a (sometimes dry) irrigation ditch and starts alternating between steep wood stair steps and steep rocky trail. After about 200 yards, you'll wonder why you're running and smartly break into a power hike.

The steepness tapers off at several places on the climb to the summit, so much so that you'll feel compelled to start running again. Pick your spots, though, because it will get very steep again. By the time you cross under the power lines, you've traveled about 1 mile. Keep chugging away for another 0.25 mile and you'll eventually reach the top.

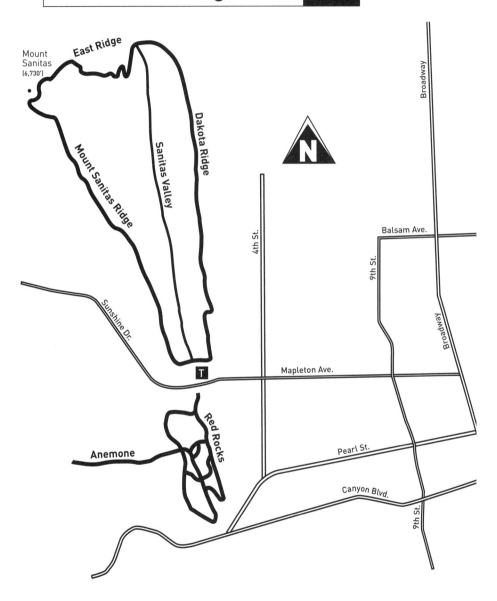

Mount Sanitas and Dakota Ridge Trail — Run 17

Mount Sanitas (6,730')

East Ridge

Dakota Ridge

Sanitas Valley

Mount Sanitas Ridge

Sunshine Dr.

4th St.

9th St.

Balsam Ave.

Broadway

Broadway

Mapleton Ave.

T

Red Rocks

Anemone

Pearl St.

Canyon Blvd.

9th St.

Once on top, take a moment to enjoy the spectacular view of Boulder and the valley below. If the other runners and hikers look like ants, it's because you're nearly 1,000 feet above them. After you've caught your breath, start carefully down the 0.9-mile descent of East Ridge, a precarious trail with plenty of places for missteps. Take your time and watch every step, because this is the last place you want to trip and fall.

About the time the trail gets wider and less steep, you'll pass a trailhead sign at the top of Sanitas Valley Trail. Follow this gravel road down about 200 yards as it curves to the right and then veer left onto a singletrack route that heads into the trees. You're now on Dakota Ridge Trail on the east flank of Sanitas Valley. This rugged 1.2-mile trail eventually meets back up with Sanitas Valley Trail, but it's more fun to run and usually less crowded than the valley route. Near the bottom of Sanitas Valley, look for a trail that angles back toward the picnic shelter.

While your ascent of Mount Sanitas will probably take you 20 to 25 minutes, a few local hotshots have run from bottom to top in a lung-bursting 14 minutes. But that's nothing. While training for the Leadville 100 in 2002, Paul Pomeroy, an ultrarunner from Lyons, Colorado, started at the trailhead picnic shelter near the main parking area and ran and power hiked up Sanitas, ran down the trail on the northeast side and then down the valley road. He completed 24 laps and 80 miles (with more than 31,000 feet of ascending) in 23 hours, 18 minutes.

Alternate Route: You can always do this loop in reverse, although it's not going to be any easier. Running up Dakota Ridge and East Ridge trails to the summit will scorch your legs and lungs just the same. To add additional time to your run, cross over Sunshine Drive (Mapleton Avenue) and run some of the steeps in Red Rocks. When you reach the trail junction at the Red Rocks saddle, go to the right and follow the 1.5-mile Anemone Trail for a challenging but especially tranquil run.

Wildlife: Deer, coyotes, foxes, skunks, mountain lions and bears.
Weather: Mount Sanitas' trails are accessible throughout the year but can be icy or muddy in the winter months—especially on the north-facing slopes of East Ridge Trail.
Other Users: Lots and lots and lots of hikers. Mountain bikes and horses are not allowed on Mount Sanitas.
Map: City of Boulder Open Space & Mountain Parks, 2002.
Contact Info: (303) 441-3440, www.ci.boulder.co.us/openspace.

Beth Reece runs away from her running partner on Anemone Trail.

South Boulder Creek Trail
Run 18

Distance/Terrain: 7 miles (round-trip) on flat, groomed, dirt and gravel paths.

Difficulty: Easy.

Elevation Change: None.

Trailheads: Park at the Bobolink trailhead at the trails' north end, near the inter-section of Baseline and Cherryvale roads. You can also park at the south end on Marshall Road just outside Boulder's southern city limits.

Dogs: Dogs are allowed only on the north portion of the trail. Dogs are prohibited from entering the south portion of the trail, because the land is an active live-stock ranch.

Jogging Strollers: Yes, the flat and smooth surfaces of the path are ideal for pushing your future runners.

Route Description: A flat out-and-back trail in southeast Boulder, South Boulder Creek Trail sees a lot of traffic, especially between Baseline Road and South Boulder Road. Typically the most crowded time is late afternoon through early evening.

Starting from the north trailhead, the trail winds southward through a grove of trees along South Boulder Creek. After about 0.5 mile, it pops out of the trees, crosses a concrete sidewalk and meanders southward adjacent to a wild grass-land. From there (mile 1.4), it turns to the east, crosses a short bridge over a drainage creek and cuts through a tunnel under South Boulder Road. When you pop out on the other side, run west about 300 yards, cross the creek and take a left through the steel gate with the Open Space sign on it. The trail runs due south for another 0.5 mile, passes under Highway 36 and continues 1.3 miles through an active cattle ranch to the south trailhead on Marshall Road (adjacent to Highway 93).

Alternate Routes: There are two easy ways to add a few miles to this run. The first is to run a 4.5-mile loop starting from the South Boulder Creek's west trail-head on Highway 93 about 0.75 miles south of the south trailhead described above. When you reach the south trailhead, run about 0.5 miles south on Marshall Road and look for a singletrack dirt trail that runs west along a private residence. Cross Highway 93 (Be very careful!) to reach the parking lot at the west trailhead. From there, head southwest for 1.9 miles on South Boulder Creek Trail on the way up to Mesa Trail (see Mesa Trail route description on page 71).

South Boulder Creek Trail Run 18

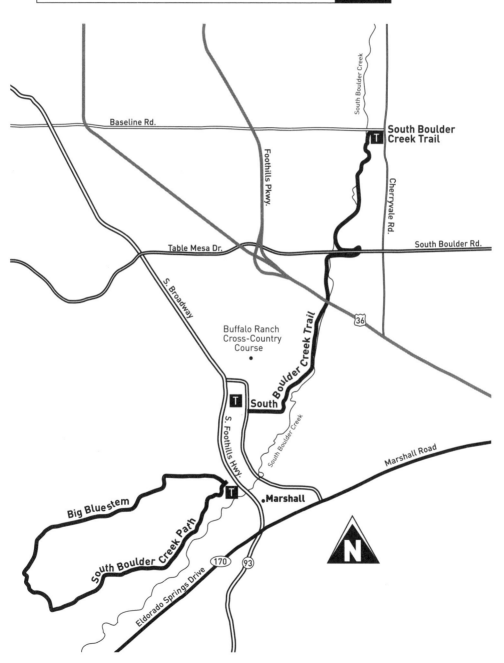

Take a right and run uphill on Mesa Trail about 400 yards to the junction with Big Bluestem Trail. Make a right at the junction, head down into a small gully, taking the right fork in the trail. Pass through a steel gate and continue 1.8 miles down Big Bluestem (which turns into a dirt road) back to the trailhead.

For another option from the south trailhead, run north along Marshall Road until you see a singletrack dirt trail entering an open field. That's the University of Colorado's South Campus property, also known as the Buffalo Ranch cross-country course, where CU's nationally ranked men's and women's cross-country teams train and race each fall. There are several unmarked loops on the property, but it's easy to add 3 to 4 miles to your run before venturing back on South Boulder Creek Trail.

Wildlife: Coyotes, foxes, deer, skunks, snakes and raptors.
Weather: The trail can be run year-round without any problem, although it can be windy on the portions of the trail south of South Boulder Road.
Other Users: Hikers, horseback riders and mountain bikers are prevalent here most of the year.
Map: City of Boulder Open Space & Mountain Parks, 2002.
Contact Info: (303) 441-3440, www.ci.boulder.co.us/openspace.

Boulder Valley Ranch Eagle Trail System
Run 19

Distance/Terrain: 6 to 15 miles (round-trip) on wide gravel and singletrack dirt trails.
Difficulty: Easy to moderate.
Elevation Change: Minimal. Other than one steep downhill, most of the trails have gentle rolling hills.
Trailheads: Foothills trailhead, northeast of Broadway–Highway 36 intersection.
Dogs: Dogs are allowed, but must be under voice and sight control at all times.
Running Strollers: The smooth lower Eagle and Sage trails in Boulder Valley Ranch are perfect for strollers, but the upper portion of Eagle Trail and its offshoots are too rocky.

Route Description: Starting from the Foothills trailhead, run north about 400 yards on the dirt road to the trail entrance just beyond the power-line poles on the

Scott Boulbol tries to keep pace with Boggs and Taz on Hidden Valley Trail.

Boulder Valley Ranch Eagle Trail System   Run 19

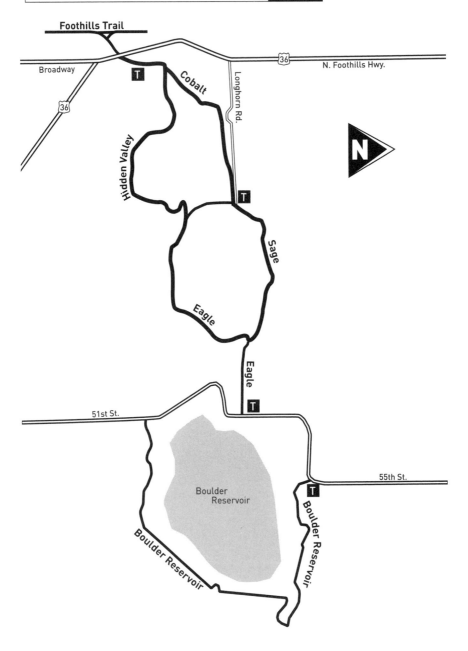

right. Once you pass the gate, run due east on Degge Trail, climb the slight hill to the top of a plateau and drop down the back side. Go right on Hidden Valley Trail as it curves southward. (If you hear gunshots, don't be alarmed—there is a privately owned shooting range located in the next valley.)

Hidden Valley Trail climbs another short hill before heading north and connecting to Mesa Reservoir Trail (mile 1.75). Go right and follow that trail for about 400 yards to the junction with Eagle Trail and take another right. Eagle Trail runs for about 0.5 mile on a high plateau, but then drops steeply down to Boulder Valley Ranch. (If you're running here at night, chances are you'll hear a pack of howling coyotes!) Once on the lower level (mile 2.5), follow Eagle Trail to the east as it winds around a small reservoir and up a small hill to an intersection with Sage Trail (mile 3.5). Hang a left on Sage Trail and follow it for 1.1 miles west through an active cattle ranch. Eagle Trail continues 0.5 miles to the east, where you can begin a 6-mile loop around Boulder Reservoir.

When you reach the Boulder Valley Ranch trailhead (mile 4.6), cross through the parking lot and continue on Sage Trail. Take an immediate right on Cobalt Trail and follow it to the west as it climbs gently to the upper level of the trail system. (Near the top of the climb, keep your eyes peeled for a circa-1930s ore smelter.) When Cobalt Trail ties into Eagle Trail (mile 5.5), take a right and follow Eagle Trail downhill and back to the first gate you passed through. Run the final 400 yards on the dirt road back to your starting point. Once back on the dirt road, jog the final 400 yards to the parking area.

Alternate Routes: There are dozens of routes that can be created from several trailheads. Another 6.5 miles can be added to the same loop by running a 6-mile loop around Boulder Reservoir via the east leg of Eagle Trail. Or park at the Lefthand trailhead (on Neva Road, east of Highway 36) or at the Lee Hill trailhead (on Lee Hill Drive west of Broadway) and develop your own routes using Foothills Trail, Hogback Ridge and Left Hand Trail. (Be sure to pick up a City of Boulder Open Space & Mountain Parks Map before you go.)

Wildlife: Coyotes, deer, fox, skunks and raptors.
Weather: Eagle Trail and adjacent routes can be run year-round, but they are quite windy at times.
Other Users: Hikers, mountain bikers and horseback riders.
Map: City of Boulder Open Space & Mountain Parks, 2002.
Contact Info: (303) 441-3440, www.ci.boulder.co.us/openspace.

Walker Ranch Loop
Run 20

Distance/Terrain: 7.6 miles (round-trip) on singletrack dirt trails.

Difficulty: Hard.

Elevation Change: Moderate to extreme. The loop is situated between 6,400 and 7,400 feet and features several long, steep climbs and descents.

Trailhead: Walker Ranch trailhead, 8 miles southwest of Boulder via Flagstaff and Kossler Lake roads.

Dogs: Yes, but dogs must be leashed at all times.

Jogging Strollers: No, definitely not. The trail is too rugged, narrow and steep.

Route Description: Even though the climbing sections of the Walker Ranch loop can be brutally hard, it is an extraordinary loop that offers stunning views, a spectacular waterfall and several fast downhill sections. But it's also one of the most popular mountain biking trails in Boulder, so you'll need stay alert to keep from getting run over by a fat-tire fiend.

To run the loop counterclockwise, start by leaving the trailhead and taking South Boulder Creek Trail to the right. The trail drops quickly for 1 mile on its way down to its namesake creek. After crossing a small brook, the trail flattens out and eventually meets up with South Boulder Creek. Run alongside the creek for about 0.5 mile, then cross the wooden bridge and get ready for action. The trail begins a twisting, 1.4-mile have-no-mercy ascent to the Crescent Meadows trailhead near the western edge of Eldorado Canyon State Park.

Continuing east, the trail rolls up and down for about 2 miles through prairie grasses and conifer forests before beginning a very steep and treacherous stair-step descent toward a spectacular South Boulder Creek waterfall. (You've run 5 rugged miles, so take a moment to enjoy the scene and splash your face with icy cold water.) From there, continue down the rocky trail, cross the large wooden and steel bridge and get ready for more climbing.

Not long after crossing the bridge, you'll come to a junction of three trails. You want to take the left flank of Eldorado Canyon Trail as it heads up Martin Gulch on a wide dirt trail. (Note: You don't want the portion of Eldorado Canyon Trail that begins a steep climb into the trees.) The way up Martin Gulch includes two rugged climbs before a refreshing downhill that takes you to a fork in the trail. Go left on Columbine Gulch Trail and begin the equally strenuous 1.6-mile climb up the gulch back to the trailhead.

Walker Ranch Loop   Run 20

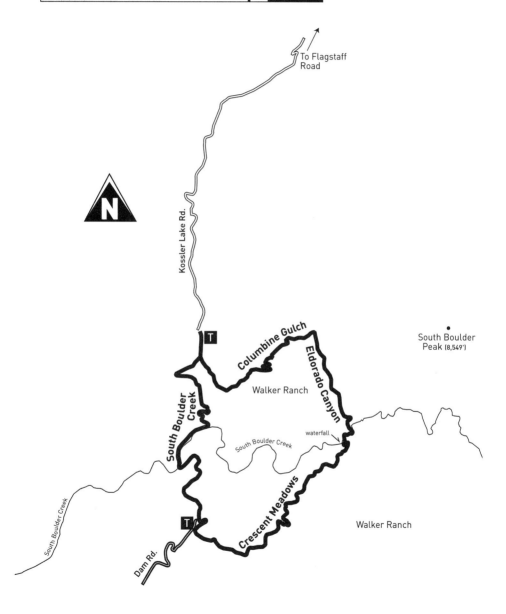

To Flagstaff Road

Kossler Lake Rd.

Columbine Gulch

Eldorado Canyon

Walker Ranch

South Boulder Creek

South Boulder Creek

waterfall

South Boulder Peak (8,549')

Crescent Meadows

Dam Rd.

Walker Ranch

South Boulder Creek

N

Wildlife: Deer, foxes, raccoons, squirrels, mountain lions, bears and trout.

Weather: Because Walker Ranch is 1,500 to 2,000 feet higher than downtown Boulder, it's typically cooler and more prone to changing conditions. The trails can be run year-round, although big snowfalls can make for treacherous conditions in many places. The north-facing slopes can hold snow well into spring, even if it has been warm and sunny in Boulder.

Other Users: Mountain bikers (Walker Ranch has some of the most popular mountain bike trails in Boulder), hikers and equestrians.

Map: City of Boulder Open Space & Mountain Parks, 2002.

Contact Info: (303) 441-3440, www.ci.boulder.co.us/openspace.

Other Boulder-area Trails

1. Fowler Trail to Rattlesnake Gulch, Eldorado Springs

Distance: 7 miles (round-trip). Difficulty: Moderate to hard. Begin at the end of County Road 67, just southeast of the town of Eldorado Springs. The trail starts as a winding dirt road and eventually sneaks into Eldorado Canyon State Park near Bastille Rock, a popular rock-climbing route. When the trail forks after about 2 miles, take the Rattlesnake Gulch spur to the left and begin a 2.0-mile lung-busting climb up Rattlesnake Gulch. Stop to see the remains of the Crags Hotel (circa 1904) and perhaps a train passing through a tunnel at the top end of the gulch. Dogs are allowed but must be leashed inside the state park.

2. Magnolia Road, Nederland

Distance: up to 12 miles (one way). Difficulty: Easy to moderate. Many world-class runners use this mostly dirt road west of Boulder to do fast-paced runs at high altitude. It's a rolling dirt road situated between 8,500 and 9,000 feet, so you're getting much more of a workout than you would for the same distance in Boulder. Drive west of Boulder on Boulder Canyon Drive until you reach Magnolia Road (on the left). Continue driving about 4 miles until the road turns to dirt and flattens out. Dogs are allowed, but should be kept on leash because of occasional vehicle traffic.

3. Settlers Park to Sunshine Canyon Trail, Boulder

Distance: 4.5 miles (round-trip). Difficulty: Easy to moderate. Starting from Settlers Park at the far west end of Pearl Street, follow the unmarked trail up and over the Red Rocks saddle. Take the unnamed wide dirt road down the back of the saddle and go left on the unmarked singletrack trail (Sunshine Canyon Trail) just before crossing the ditch. The trail rolls through the trees along Sunshine Drive and ends at a driveway after about 1.75 miles. Dogs are allowed but must be under voice and sight control.

4. Poorman Road Loop, Boulder

Distance: 11.0 miles (round-trip). Difficulty: Hard. Follow directions for the run listed above and when the trail ends, run up steep Sunshine Drive (paved) 2 miles to Poorman Road (dirt and gravel). Follow Poorman 2.3 miles as it winds (and dramatically drops) down to Fourmile Canyon Drive (paved). Take a left on Fourmile and run 2 miles along the shoulder to the intersection with Canyon Drive (Highway 119) and the end of Boulder Creek Path (dirt and gravel). Run 2.2 miles down Boulder Creek Path back into Boulder. Take a left over the first bridge in Eben G. Fine Park and go through the tunnel to get back to Settlers Park. Dogs are allowed but must be under voice and sight control.

5. Sourdough Trail, Nederland

Distance: 11.6 miles (round-trip). Difficulty: Moderate to Hard. A remote trail north of Nederland, this singletrack route is revered by mountain bikers, but it's typically not very crowded, even on weekends. Drive about 3 miles north of Nederland on Highway 7 (Peak to Peak Highway) to Rainbow Lakes Road and look for trailhead signs. Sourdough Trail is an out-and-back run through aspen groves and conifer forests with occasional viewpoints on the way to Brainard Lake Drive. The trail ranges between 9,000 feet and 10,200 feet has a few good climbs. Dogs are allowed but must be under voice and sight control. For more details, call the Boulder office of the U.S. Forest Service at (303) 541-2500.

6. Behind the Rocks Loop, Boulder

Distance: 22 miles (round-trip). Difficulty: Hard. This is a spectacular four- to six-hour training run that circles Green Mountain and Bear Peak. Starting from Chautauqua Park, run west up Gregory Canyon and skirt the north flank of Green Mountain on Long Trail. When you pop out on Flagstaff Road, continue on the Road (which will turn into Kossler Lake Road) until you reach the Walker Ranch Trailhead. Follow Columbine Gulch Trail to Eldorado Canyon Trail through Eldorado Canyon State Park. Run east about a mile on Eldorado Springs Drive to the south Mesa Trailhead. Return to Chautauqua Park on Mesa Trail.

Boulder's Boldest

Boulder has long been home to some extraordinary runners. **Frank Shorter** started the trend in 1970, when he decided to make Boulder his part-time training home as he pursued a berth on the 1972 Olympic team on a full-time basis. He not only won the marathon at the 1972 Olympics, he also started a running store and running apparel company and helped young U.S. runners get the opportunity to earn money and make a living by pushing for landmark changes in U.S. amateur athletic policies.

Shorter moved to Boulder permanently in 1975 and went on to earn a silver medal in the 1976 Olympic marathon (although 1976 gold-medal winner Waldemar Cierpinski of East Germany was later convicted of using performance-enhancing drugs). Many running historians credit Shorter's Olympic efforts for sparking the first recreational running boom of the 1970s.

He also created a boom in Boulder as one of the founders of the Bolder Boulder Memorial Day 10k in 1979. The race has become the fourth-largest in the U.S., with more than 45,000 participants annually. Shorter still lives in Boulder and can be seen running the trails around town from time to time.

Other top runners that followed Shorter's lead and moved to Boulder on a part-time or permanent basis include **Benji Durden** (1980 U.S. Olympic marathon trials), Australia's **Rob de Castella** (1983 winner of the marathon world championships), Mexico's **Arturo Barrios** (10,000-meter world-record holder), South Africa's **Mark Plaatjes** (1993 winner of the marathon world championships) and New Zealand's **Lorraine Moller** (1992 Olympic marathon bronze medalist).

"I came here on vacation and fell in love with this place," says Plaatjes, a physical therapist and co-owner of the Boulder Running Company stores. "The natural beauty of the place is combined with the great trails and the great support system. There are a lot of medical facilities and doctors and resources here, and everybody caters to the athletes and makes them feel special."

More than 25 years after Shorter's arrival, the Boulder area is still a hub for elite runners and endurance athletes of all types. In recent years, the local headliners have been **Colleen de Reuck** of South Africa (road-racing champion), **Uta Pippig** of Germany (Boston Marathon winner), **Silvio Guerra** of Ecuador (Boston Marathon runner-up), **Mark** and **Gwyn Coogan** (U.S. Olympians), **Chad Ricklefs** (two-time Leadville Trail 100 winner and U.S. 100k road champion), **Dan Browne** (five-time U.S. road-

Photo by Phil Mislinski/www.pmimage.com

Colleen de Reuck on her way to a strong finish in the Bolder Boulder in 2001.

racing champion), **Adam Goucher** (NCAA champion, U.S. Olympian), **Alan Culpepper** (NCAA champion, U.S. Olympian), **Dave Mackey** (trail-racing champion), **Dave Scott** (six-time Hawaii Ironman winner), **Siri Lindley** (world-champion triathlete), **Tim DeBoom** (two-time Hawaii Ironman winner) and adventure racer **Ian Adamson** (three-time Eco-Challenge winner), not to mention numerous world-class runners from Japan, Kenya, Australia, Mexico, Italy, Romania and other countries around the globe.

Some have stayed and remained part of the local running scene, some have moved on to run elsewhere, but they all have played a part in reinforcing Boulder's legend as one of the world's greatest places to run.

Boulder Road Runners Keep on Running

Where can you find the best breakfast spread in Boulder? Would you believe in the parking lot of a bank?

Sure, there are plenty of restaurants in town to get a good breakfast on a Sunday morning. But to really do it Boulder-style, you need to join the Boulder Road Runners at the bank parking lot at 30th Street and Iris Avenue.

They've been meeting there for a quiet morning run every Sunday for nearly 20 years. After the run, which typically draws 20 to 100 people and lasts 60 to 75 minutes, the group enjoys bagels, cinnamon rolls, cookies, muffins and refreshments over good conversation.

The club boasts about 500 members from all walks of life—teachers, lawyers, carpenters, therapists, coaches, entrepreneurs and electricians —with the common bonds are running and a love of Boulder.

"We try to have a lot of fun together," says Rich Castro, the club's president and one of its founders. "Running is something you can have for the rest of your life. There is more to running than just you. If you're a runner, especially in this community, you're a part of something bigger."

As far as clubs go, the group is among the most active in Boulder. Since the group's inception in 1979, its members have logged thousands of miles together, put on dozens of running events and played a huge role in the Boulder community.

Boulder Road Runners holds several races every year, including the July 4 5k, CU Kickoff Classic 5k in September, High Five Road Race in October and CU Turkey Trot in November. Proceeds from the Kickoff Classic go to the CU cross-country program, while the CU Turkey Trot and July 4 5k benefit Community Food Share.

The Boulder Road Runners also work closely with Bolder Boulder's organizers and often extend their homes to visiting world-class runners. When it comes to competitive running, the Boulder Road Runners have had their fair share of success, placing in various national club cross-country meets and road-race championships and owning a few world records. Several club members, including Patty Murray, Rick Bruess and Laura Bruess, among others, regularly place highly in local road races and at masters (older than 40) events around the country.

Another of the club's original members, Pearl Mehl, held several age-group world records when she passed away in 2002 at age 88. Not only did she set 80-and-older records for the 400-meter (2:25:03) and 1,500-meter (12:37:13), but she was also a three-time winner at the 1996 National Masters Indoor Track Championships.

The Boulder Road Runners also holds a world record for the rarely competed 10 x 10k relay race. In celebration of his 40th birthday in 1998, Andrew Crook gathered a few of the faster BRR members and set out to break the record of 6 hours, 30 minutes, 1 second set by a German club in 1994. Amid gray skies, chilly temperatures and occasional rain, the Boulder Road Runners team (five men, five women) obliterated the previous mark with a 6:03:48 effort.

"Boulder Road Runners has such a wide range of people," says BRR administrator Connie Harmon, also a group founder. "I think what's so interesting is that we have college students and we have seniors who are 70 and 80 years old who are competing. We have a good base of recreational runners who run just for the enjoyment and not necessarily trying to win races. I think it's really exciting to see so many people with a similar interest."

The Boulder Road Runners encourages new runners to join its Sunday morning runs Sunday at 9 A.M. at the First National Bank of Colorado near 30th Street and Iris Avenue. (The meeting time changes to 8 A.M. in the spring and summer.) Visit www.boulderroadrunners.org for more details.

Boulder Running Resources

Track Facilities

When it comes to speed training, there are four track facilities in Boulder. The best of the bunch is the brand-new, eight-lane Mondo track at Potts Field on the east campus of the University of Colorado. The track was rebuilt in 2002, and now it's one of the premier facilities in the state. (As of spring 2003, the University of Colorado was allowing the public to run on the track only on Tuesdays but, that policy will likely change.)

The CU track can be crowded at times, especially Tuesday afternoons and evenings. On any given Tuesday, you might see Olympians, All-American collegiate runners or a wide range of dedicated running clubs doing workouts there. The Boulder Road Runners hosts track meets there every summer (see page 93) as well as a few other events.

* University of Colorado, Potts Field, located north of Colorado Avenue and 33rd Street
* University of Colorado, Balch Fieldhouse (indoor track), on the CU campus east of Folsom Field
* Fairview High School, 1515 Greenbriar
* Boulder High School, 1604 Arapahoe Avenue

Group Runs

Boulder Road Runners

The club meets at 8 A.M. (9 A.M. in winter) on Sunday mornings at the First National Bank of Colorado, 3033 Iris Avenue. New runners of all abilities are encouraged to run. Visit www.boulderroadrunners.org for more details or send an e-mail to webmaster@boulderroadrunners.org

Boulder Striders/Running Republic

This club trains for a variety of races, including the Bolder Boulder.
(303) 579-0870; kwazulu11@msn.com

Boulder Trail Runners

The group typically meets Thursdays at 5:30 P.M. at Chautauqua Park, rain, snow or shine. New runners of all abilities are encouraged to run. For details, visit http://groups.yahoo.com/group/BoulderTrailRunners or send an e-mail to bouldertrailrunners@yahoogroups.com

The CU track team typically hosts one or two meets per year on its outdoor track. The Potts Track Series is held on the same track every summer.

Fleet Feet Sports Running Group

Both male and female members meet at 1035 Pearl Street, Suite 100, Mondays at 6:15 P.M.; the women's group meets Wednesdays at 6:15 P.M. New runners of all abilities are encouraged to run. Visit www.fleetfeet.com/events/19 for details, or call (303) 939-8000.

Potts Track Series

The Boulder Road Runners sponsors a community track meet series at the Potts Field track on the University of Colorado campus every summer, with events ranging from 100 meters to 5,000 meters, as well as long jump, high jump and shot put. Meets are typically held on the first and third Thursday of June, July and August and begin promptly at 6 P.M.

Resources

BoulderRunning.com

A new website aimed at creating an online community for the Boulder running scene, it will have news stories, race results, training tips and more. www.BoulderRunning.com

Like clockwork, the Boulder Trail Runners begin a Thursday night run from Chautauqua trailhead.

Running Retailers

Active Endeavors

1122 Pearl St.

(303) 448-1770

www.activeendeavors.com

Active Imprints

629 S. Broadway

(303) 494-0321

Boulder Running Company

2775 Pearl St., #103

(303) 786-9255

www.boulderrunningcompany.com

Eastern Mountain Sports

2550 Arapahoe Ave.

(303) 442-7566

www.ems.com

Fleet Feet Sports
1035 Pearl St., Suite 100
(303) 939-8000
www.fleetfeet.com

Mountain Sports
2835 Pearl St.
(303) 442-8355
www.mospo.com

Outdoor Divas
1133 Pearl St.
(303) 449-3482

REI
1789 28th St.
(303) 583-9970
www.rei.com

Runners Choice
2460 Canyon Blvd.
(303) 449-8551

Speed demon Jason Smith and his dog, Izzy, blaze the trail at Matthews/Winters
Park in Morrison.

Front Range West

Golden, Morrison, Evergreen, Idaho Springs, Lakewood and Littleton

The foothills west of Denver near the communities of Golden, Lakewood, Morrison, Evergreen and Idaho Springs have an abundance of running trails managed by a variety of land agencies. The region has a diverse topography, ranging from gentle dirt trails in Bear Creek Lake Park to the 14,264-foot summit of Mount Evans. The common denominators for all the routes in this section are an intrinsic beauty and an unpolished ruggedness decidedly removed from urban chaos. While many of the trails can get crowded on weekends, most are virtually bare during the week. "Whenever I need to get away for a good trail run, I drive due west and kind of figure out where I'm going to run on the way there," says Lakewood resident and 3:17 marathoner Tom Welton. "There are just too many trails and not enough time."

Apex Park Run 21

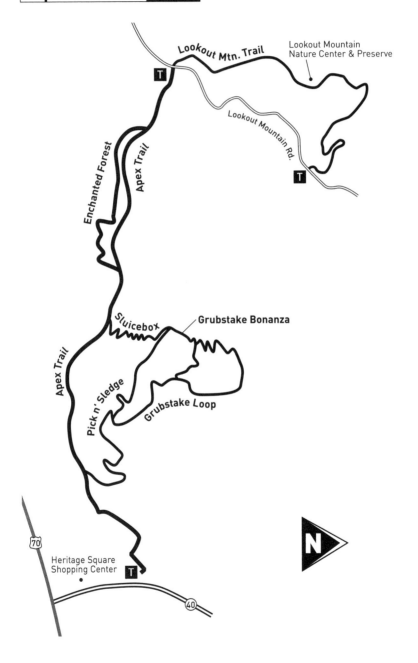

Apex Park (Golden)
Run 21

Distance/Terrain: 6.0 to 10.0 miles on dirt singletrack trails.
Difficulty: Moderate.
Elevation Change: Moderate to extreme. The main trail climbs about 1,800 feet in
2.8 miles from the Heritage Square parking lot to Lookout Mountain Road.
Trailhead: Park in the northern edge of the Heritage Square Shopping Center
located on Highway 40 at County Road 93. The trail starts on the other side of
the wooden fence bordering the parking lot.
Dogs: Dogs must be on a leash at all times.
Running Strollers: Not advised. The trail is both too narrow and too steep to bring
the baby along on this one.

Route Description: Get ready to go up! Like many of the trails on the edge of the
foothills, Apex Trail starts with a long, gradual climb. It begins with a mild ascent
from the parking lot, but starts to get steeper after about 0.7 mile. As you start to
rise, you can get a bird's-eye view of the 1880s-themed Heritage Square, complete
with a quilt museum and miniature railroad. You'll soon pass a sign that explains
the history of Apex Gulch, including how a toll road through the gulch once led to
the gold mines in Central City. Don't dwell on the historical aspects too much,
otherwise you might get clobbered by a downhill mountain biker and wind up
being history yourself.

The exposed trail continues a gradual ascent through the gulch, varying in
degrees of steepness as it winds toward Lookout Mountain Road. There are several
trail offshoots, but stay on the main trail on the way up and catch the alternate
routes on the way down. Regardless of the trail you're on, keep your eyes peeled
for mountain bikers and equestrians. A collision with either one could leave a permanent mark. At the top of Apex Gulch (mile 2.8), you'll leave Apex Park and reach
Lookout Mountain Road and a junction with Lookout Mountain Trail (see below).
On the way down the Gulch, take in views of Golden and Denver on the eastern
horizon and get ready for a screamin' downhill run. Take the right fork about 0.3
mile from the top and zigzag down the heavily wooded Enchanted Forest Trail. It's
only 1.3 miles long and it connects back into the Apex Trail about 1.0 mile from the
top, but it's a fun diversion that's almost completely shaded. Once back on Apex
Trail, continue to the parking lot to complete an exhausting 6.2-mile run.

Alternate Routes: For additional mileage (and more climbing), on your way

Pam Simich and her exhausted dog, Boggs, finish a run at Apex Park near Golden.

down Apex Trail hang a left on Sluicebox Trail, about 1.3 miles down from the top of Apex Gulch. Sluicebox is a steep series of switchbacks that ties into the Grubstake Loop on Indian Mountain. The Sluicebox–Grubstake–Sluicebox round-trip adds only 1.6 miles, but several variations are possible on the Pick n' Sledge and Bonanza trails. It's also possible to start an Apex Park run from the Lookout Mountain Nature Center (see the "Chimney Gulch and Lookout Mountain" write-up in the Other Trails section on page 131) off Lookout Mountain Road northwest of Apex Park. Lookout Mountain Trail is a mile long and connects with Apex Trail at the top of the park.

Wildlife: Deer, foxes, raccoons, squirrels, skunks, a variety of birds and very rarely bears.
Weather: With the exception of the Enchanted Forest segment, most of the trails in Apex Park are vulnerable to high winds and extended exposure to the sun in the summer months. From late fall to early spring, Apex Trail can be muddy and often shrouded in shade.
Other Users: Hikers, mountain bikers, horseback riders and bird-watchers.
Map: Apex Park Map, Jefferson County Open Space, 2002.
Contact Info: (303) 271-5925, http://openspace.co.jefferson.co.us.

Bear Creek Lake Park (Lakewood)
Run 22

Distance/Terrain: 3.0 to 9.0 miles (depending on route) on singletrack dirt trails, paved roads and concrete bike paths.
Difficulty: Easy to moderate.
Elevation Change: Minimal to moderate.
Trailhead: The park entrance is at 15600 West Morrison Rd. (Route 8), about a quarter-mile east of the C-470 freeway. A $4 fee per vehicle ($3 for seniors) applies at all times. Public restrooms are located throughout the park, including at the visitor center about a 0.5 mile south of the main entrance.
Dogs: Yes, you can bring your pup, but it must be kept on a leash at all times.
Running Strollers: Not recommended, unless you run the paved roads and concrete sidewalks. The dirt trails aren't conducive to stroller wheels.

Route Description: Located just east of Bear Canyon, 2,600-acre Bear Creek Lake

Bear Creek Lake Park   Run 22

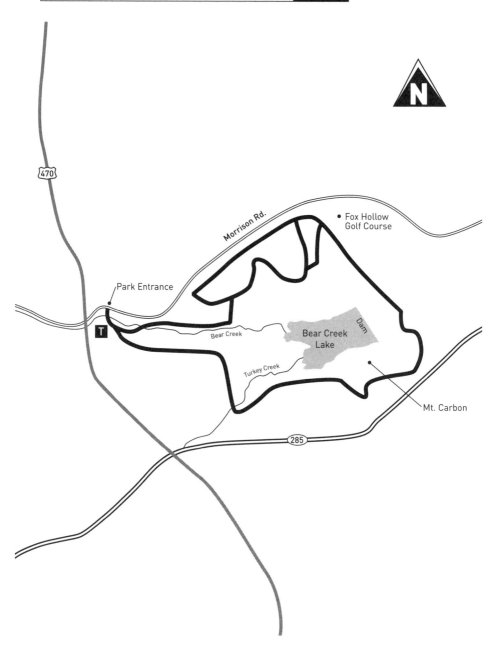

Park is the largest park in Lakewood. It offers a variety of paved and dirt trails, all with views of the foothills to the west and Green Mountain Park (see Run 25 on page 110) to the north. It's an ideal place for long, slow Sunday runs (on mostly flat terrain) or fartlek-type workouts on a variety of sparsely frequented routes.

After driving through the main entrance, continue about 200 yards, take a right and cross Bear Creek. Veer to your right and park in the Skunk Hollow picnic area. From there, locate the dirt horse trail in the woods near the creek and begin running to the east (downstream). The horse trail crosses the road and then ducks back into the woods along the south side of the creek. After about 1.5 miles, you'll see nearby Bear Creek Lake, a reservoir formed by Turkey Creek, Bear Creek and Mount Carbon Dam. Cross to the north side of the creek near the Whitetail picnic area and continue northeast on the horse trail as it parallels the park road and begins ascending toward the top of Mount Carbon Dam. The trail tops out near the northern edge of the dam and then begins a steep descent into Fox Hollow Golf Course on the back side of the dam.

Follow the trail along the edge of the public links for about 1.0 mile, eventually passing a golf course maintenance building. Look for the paved path that continues up the south side of the dam, and get ready to huff and puff on the way up. The route eventually pops out on the back side of Mount Carbon, a 5,770-foot hill just south of Bear Creek Lake.

From there, pick up the concrete bike path and follow it as it slopes downhill to the west for about 1.0 mile, crossing a bridge over Turkey Creek at the bottom of the swell. Follow the bike path as it passes through the Indian Paintbrush Campground and follow it westward to the Soda Lake Marina. From there, it's about a 0.25 mile to the visitor center (where there is a drinking fountain, just in case you're thirsty) and another half-mile back to the Skunk Hollow picnic area to complete a 6.0-mile loop.

Alternate Routes: Several other park paths, including the short Fitness Trail, head out to Pelican Point on the west side of the lake. There are also several other horse trails in the hilly terrain near the park's northern boundary.

Wildlife: Deer, coyotes, snakes, prairie dogs, elk, bald eagles and a variety of birds, waterfowl and fish.
Weather: The park is open year-round with park hours varying according to the season. The upper, exposed areas of the park can be windy, but the horse trail along the creek is protected from all types of inclement weather.
Other Users: Hikers, bikers, swimmers, boating enthusiasts, equestrians and picnickers.
Map: Bear Creek Lake Park Map, City of Lakewood.
Contact Info: (303) 697-6159, www.lakewood.org.

Evergreen Lake Loop and deDisse Park (Evergreen)
Run 23

Distance/Terrain: About 1.5 miles per loop around Evergreen Lake on a combination of gravel-and-dirt trails and concrete bike paths.

Difficulty: Easy.

Elevation Change: Minimal, except for the short stair climbs near the dam at the east end of the lake.

Trailheads: The two obvious places to park are at the deDisse Park trailhead along Highway 74 or the parking lot of the log boathouse at the west end of the lake. Public restrooms are available at the boathouse.

Dogs: Yes, dogs are allowed, but they must be on a leash at all times.

Running Strollers: Not advised, unless you want to carry it down and up a flight of stairs on every lap.

Route Description: Evergreen Lake Loop is a gravel trail that circles Evergreen Lake, a 55-acre reservoir situated about 2.0 miles west of the town of Evergreen. While it's a pretty basic trail, the presence of the calm lake gives this loop one of the most serene 1.5-mile sections of trail anywhere along the Front Range. It's a great place to run slow, methodical miles, but just as ideal for quick fartlek (interval) workouts.

Starting from the boathouse, follow the trail south to the lake's southern bank. The route continues along a bluff high above the water, eventually coming to a fork. Take the left fork, cross a short bridge and head north onto the paved road. Continue down the road until you reach a dirt trail on your left. Follow the trail along the edge of the lake until you get to the south side of the 35-foot dam on the east end of the lake. Climb down the stairs, cross three short bridges spanning the dam spillway and climb up the stairs on the north side of the dam. Once you're back at the level of the lake, follow the trail as it parallels Highway 74. The final 0.5 mile back to the boathouse includes several footbridges over a protected wetland.

Alternate Routes: Several other dirt singletrack trails are accessible from Evergreen Lake Loop, including many routes in the adjacent deDisse Park and Alderfer/Three Sisters Park (for a description, see the "Other Trails" section on page 130).

Wildlife: Deer, skunks, raccoons, foxes, coyotes, squirrels, snakes and fish.

Weather: The trail is accessible year-round, but it can be severely windy at times.

Evergreen Lake Loop and deDisse Park Run 23

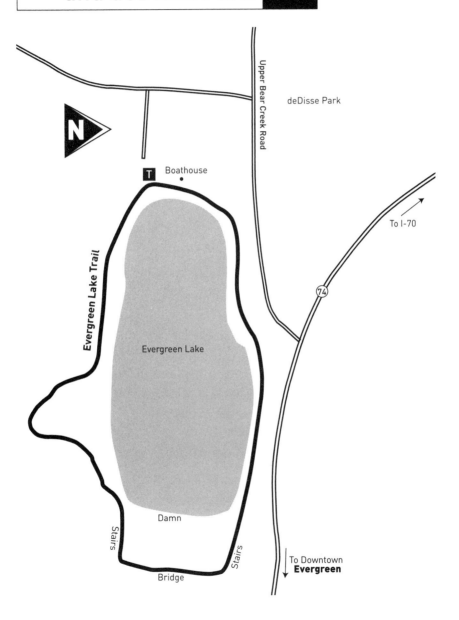

The short loop around Evergreen Lake is as relaxing as it gets.

Other Users: Hikers, bikers, fishermen, boating enthusiasts and swimmers.

Map: deDisse Park, Denver Mountain Parks; Evergreen Park and Recreation District.

Contact Info: (303) 512-9300, www.denvergov.org/Mountain_Parks.

Elk Meadow Park (Evergreen)
Run 24

Distance/Terrain: 5.0 to 12.0 miles on soft, singletrack trails.

Difficulty: Easy to hard. Most trails have mildly rolling hills, but the route to the top of Bergen Peak is grueling.

Elevation Change: Meadow View Trail gradually gains about 250 feet from the main trailhead; Bergen Peak Trail climbs a whopping 1,730 feet.

Trailheads: The main parking area is at Evergreen Parkway (Highway 74) and Lewis Ridge Road; another trailhead is located about 1.0 mile west of Evergreen Parkway on Stagecoach Boulevard. (Take 1-70 west into the foothills to Exit 252 and head south on Highway 74.) Public restrooms are available at both trailheads.

Dogs: Allowed, but they must be on a leash at all times.

Running Strollers: Not recommended on these narrow and undulating single-track trails.

Route Description: Elk Meadow Park's 5.0-mile loop—the Sleepy S, Meadow View and Painters Pause trails—is a short but satisfying singletrack route on property that was used primarily for cattle ranching from 1905 to 1977. Half of the trail tunnels through dense forest, while the other half cuts through open prairie.

Starting from the Lewis Ridge Road parking lot, pick up Sleepy S Trail and follow it as it curves around to the south, climbing slowly for 1.0 mile or so. Bypass Elk Ridge Trail and continue as Sleepy S takes makes a hairpin turn to the right and continues climbing to the intersection with Meadow View Trail. Take a right at the trail junction and continue on Meadow View Trail as it hugs a ridgeline thickly forested with lodgepole pine. (Ignore the junction with Bergen Peak Trail.) When you pass through an open meadow and cross the wooden bridge over Bergen Creek, you're at the halfway point of this loop. Continue as the trail rides the ridgeline (past the intersection with Too Long Trail) and follow it as it descends past a stone shelter all the way to Painters Pause Trail along Highway 74. You can take a right on Painter's Pause Trail and follow the remaining 1.0 mile or so back

Elk Meadow Park Run 24

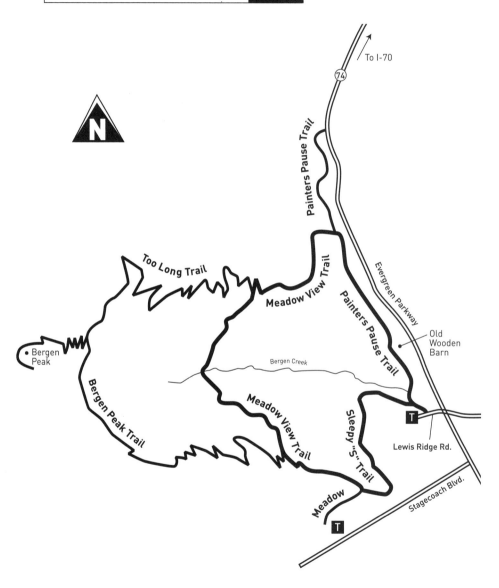

to the parking lot (passing the early-20th-century wooden barn along the way), for a run totaling 5.0 miles. Or you can lengthen your run by 1.5 miles by taking a left on Painters Pause and running northward to the edge of the park property and back before heading to your car.

Alternate Routes: If you're up for a little bit of uphill running, take the Bergen Peak summit extension, which connects to Meadow View Trail at two points (Note: The south connection is called the Bergen Peak Trail, while the north connection is called Too Long Trail, but both are about the same length.) The route to Bergen Peak and back via the Bergen Peak Trail is about 7.25 miles, which would make your run from the Lewis Ridge parking lot almost 12.5 miles if you continued with the remainder of the trail described above. Regardless of where you start, you're in for about 1.0 mile and half of steep switch-backing trails and 1,730 feet of elevation gain to the summit. The trail eventually levels out, but just when you've caught your breath, you'll be at the junction of the summit trail, which will send you up another steep 1.0-mile jaunt to 9,700-foot Bergen Peak. The panoramic vista from the top makes it all worthwhile, as does the forested downhill return to Meadow View Trail.

Wildlife: Coyotes, deer, raccoons, bears, mountain lions, foxes, skunks and prairie dogs.
Weather: The lower sections of Elk Meadow Park, especially the Painters Pause, Founders and Sleepy S trails, can be very windy because of the gusts coming over the top of Bergen Peak. The trails are typically snowy and slippery most of the winter and often muddy in the spring.
Other Users: Mountain bikers, hikers and artists.
Map: Elk Meadow Park Map, Jefferson County Open Space Department.
Contact Info: (303) 271-5975, http://openspace.co.jefferson.co.us.

Green Mountain Park Run 25

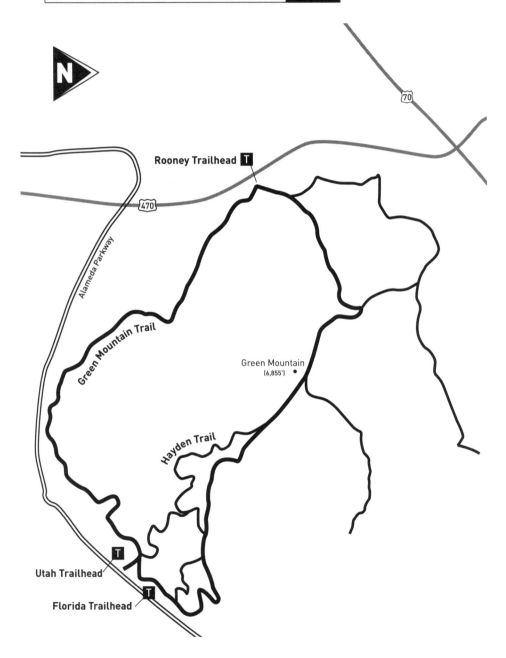

N

Rooney Trailhead T

Alameda Parkway

Green Mountain Trail

Green Mountain
(6,855')

Hayden Trail

Utah Trailhead T

Florida Trailhead T

Green Mountain Park (Lakewood)
Run 25

Distance/Terrain: 6.5 (round-trip) on technical singletrack and wide dirt trails.

Difficulty: Hard. The climbs are short but steep, and filled with loose rocks and gravel in many places.

Elevation Change: Moderate to extreme. The Green Mountain Trail climbs 600 to 800 feet from the main trailhead to the 6,855-foot summit of Green Mountain.

Trailheads: There are three primary trailheads that offer equal access to the Green Mountain loop: the Utah trailhead, on the southeast corner of the park on Alameda Parkway; the Florida trailhead, also on the southeast corner of the park on Alameda Parkway; and the Rooney trailhead, off Rooney Road on the west side of C-470. Public restrooms are available near the Utah trailhead at the Green Mountain Recreation Center (on the south side of Alameda Parkway).

Dogs: Yes, dogs are allowed but they must be kept on a leash at all times.

Running Strollers: Are you nuts? It's hard enough running this loop without any accessories. Besides, the trail isn't conducive to strollers.

Route Description: One of the steepest and most challenging routes east of C-470, this is a good place to do some hill training. Strong legs, strong lungs and a good attitude will go a long way on the treeless 6.5-mile Green Mountain Trail loop, because you're bound to get your share of climbing and wind, whether you like it or not.

From the Utah trailhead, take the short connector trail to the Green Mountain Trail loop, then go left to start the loop in a clockwise direction and follow the trail to the west. The undulating singletrack twists and turns without much elevation change for about 2.75 miles to the western edge of the park, where it intersects with a trail leading to the Rooney trailhead. But in the 0.75 mile beyond the junction with the Rooney trailhead offshoot, the Green Mountain Trail soars 800 feet in a lung-busting, thigh-burning climb on a dirt road to the summit. When you reach a fork in the trail (mile 3.5), take the right fork and continue a moderate climb to the peak. You'll certainly need to catch your breath, so be sure to take in the extraordinary views in all directions: Denver's skyline to the east, the buttes of Golden to the north, Pikes Peak to the south and Mount Falcon and Mount Evans to the west.

It's almost all downhill from here. The trail descends gradually for about 1.2 miles as it follows the summit ridgeline but then drops dramatically in the final 1.5 miles toward the Florida trailhead. After coming to the junction with the Florida trailhead spur, go right and continue down the trail for about 0.5 mile as Green

Mountain Trail parallels Alameda Parkway and takes you to the fork (go straight ahead) leading back to the Utah trailhead (mile 6.5).

Alternate Routes: There are several other trails adjacent to the Green Mountain Trail loop, although some lead away from the trail to residential areas on the northeast side of the mountain. The only other prominently marked trail is Hayden Trail, which actually short-cuts out of the southeast corner of the Green Mountain loop and goes directly back to the Utah trailhead.

Wildlife: Deer, black-tailed prairie dogs, silver and red foxes, coyotes, bull snakes and hawks are the most prevalent, although mountain lions and rattlesnakes have also been spotted there.

Weather: Exposure to wind is the most common problem, as high gusts (seemingly from all directions) are prevalent, especially on the top and west sides of the mountain. The trails can be slippery in winter, but they're typically not too muddy in spring.

Other Users: Hikers, mountain bikers, paragliders and equestrians.

Map: City of Lakewood Parks, Open Space and Facilities, 2002.

Contact Info: (303) 987-7800, www.lakewood.org.

Matthews/Winters Park (Morrison)
Run 26

Distance/Terrain: A 6.0- to 6.5-mile loop on singletrack dirt trails and gravel fire roads, depending on the route chosen.

Difficulty: Moderate.

Elevation Change: Minimal to moderate. There are several moderate climbs on the park's Red Rocks/Dakota Ridge loop, no matter which direction you run.

Trailhead: Matthews/Winters Park trailhead, located on Colorado Highway 26, just south of the I-70 Morrison exit. A public restroom is available near the trailhead.

Dogs: Yes, you can run with your pooch as long as it's on a leash.

Running Strollers: Nope, it's not an option on these undulating, rock-strewn trails.

Route Description: The Red Rocks–Dakota Ridge loop offers a wide variety of trails, expansive views and, if you're lucky, a chance to hear your favorite band live in concert at nearby Red Rocks Amphitheater.

Starting from the main trailhead, begin the loop in a counterclockwise direction

Matthews/Winters Park `Run 26`

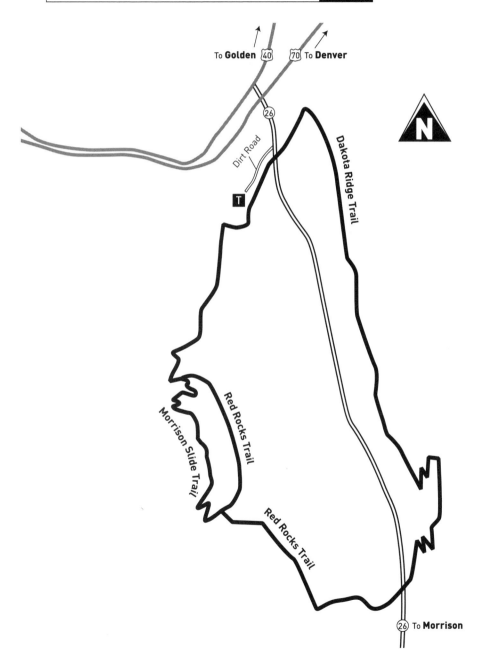

by heading south on Red Rocks Trail. After a short climb, the trail follows a ridgeline for about 1.0 mile before coming to its first junction with Morrison Slide Trail (see Alternate Routes below). Red Rocks Trail is the lower route that bears left. It continues along a ridgeline for almost 1.0 mile, then bends around some unique red rock buttresses as it begins dropping in elevation. (The Morrison Slide Trail reconnects with Red Rocks Trail here.) Red Rocks Trail continues a slow descent, crosses a road and then winds through a grassy field before popping out on a road near Highway 26 (mile 3.0).

Be careful as you cross the highway; traffic is typically moving fast in both directions. Dakota Ridge Trail begins on the east side of the road, slightly to the south of where Red Rocks Trail meets the highway. From there, the trail climbs steeply for 0.5-mile to the back side of Dakota Ridge. (It can be a real grind, but don't knock yourself out because the hardest climb is yet to come!) The trail pops out on a paved road overlooking the C-470 freeway and Denver's western suburbs. Cross at the crosswalk painted on the road and begin what will be a rather grueling 2.0-mile climb up the hogback ridgeline of Dakota Ridge. The trail is very rocky, and just when you think you've reach the summit, you wind up climbing again. When you've finally crested the last point, you'll begin a quick and rewarding 0.5-mile descent back to the Matthews/Winters Park trailhead. Upon your return, you will have completed a challenging 6.0-mile loop.

Alternate Routes: The Morrison Slide Trail is a 1.2-mile parallel route off of Red Rocks Trail. It can add about 0.5 mile to the entire loop, but it includes about 580 feet of climbing, so it will feel like more than that. After ascending a series of switchbacks, you'll be rewarded with stunning views to the east and a relatively flat ridge run and then a steep descent through some interesting red rock formations near the south junction with Red Rocks Trail.

Wildlife: Deer, foxes, squirrels, prairie dogs, coyotes, snakes and hawks.
Weather: The trails in the western side of the park (Red Rocks and Morrison Slide trails) are protected from the wind but can be slippery and muddy in late winter and spring. The rocky Dakota Ridge Trail is exposed to high winds but is rarely muddy.
Other Users: Hikers, mountain bikers and equestrians.
Map: Matthews/Winters Park Map, Jefferson County Open Space, 2002.
Contact Info: (303) 271-5925, http://openspace.co.jefferson.co.us.

Maxwell Falls Trail (Evergreen)
Run 27

Distance/Terrain: 9.0 miles (round-trip) on soft singletrack forest trails.

Difficulty: Moderate. The trail has many rolling hills and a few steep climbs.

Elevation Change: Moderate.

Trailheads: There are two U.S. Forest Service trailheads. The lower trailhead is located just south of Morrison on Brook Forest Road about 3.0 miles west of Highway 73. The upper trailhead is about 3.0 miles farther down Brook Forest Road near the foot of the dam on Stevenson Reservoir. There are public restrooms at the upper trailhead, but not at the lower trailhead.

Dogs: Yes, dogs are allowed, but must be under voice and sight control at all times.

Running Strollers: Nope. You'll never be able to push a stroller on this route.

Route Description: An idyllic and often sparsely populated trail, Maxwell Falls Trail is a perfect way to escape hot summer afternoons—especially if you decide to run all the way to the falls. The waterfall's flow is greatest between late March and early May, a period when high-altitude snowpack is quickly melting. Most of the trail is sheltered by thick pine forest, offering a perfect canopy from the beating sun. Regardless of which trailhead you start from, the trail is primarily an up-and-down, out-and-back run.

Starting from the lower trailhead, the trail starts with a couple of moderately steep inclines, but don't fret—it gets easier after the first mile or so. After coming to a clearing and an intersection with another trail (ignore that trail and run straight ahead!), the trail starts a mild descent back into the woods. At the bottom of the gully, the twisting and turning trail follows Maxwell Creek upstream for about 2.0 miles to the intersection with the upper trailhead. Along the way, you pass through a dense forest that includes a variety of conifers, deciduous trees and aspen groves.

From the upper trailhead, you've got about another 1.5 miles to Maxwell Falls—the reason you decided to run this trail in the first place. From the parking lot, run up the road on the right side of the dam and reservoir. The trail resumes beyond the reservoir and alternates between modest climbs and mild descents until it splits near the falls; follow the narrow footpath to the left to reach the base of the falls, where you can reward yourself with a splash of cold water on your face. Turn around and head back the way you came to complete and extremely satisfying 9.0-mile run.

Maxwell Falls Trail Run 27

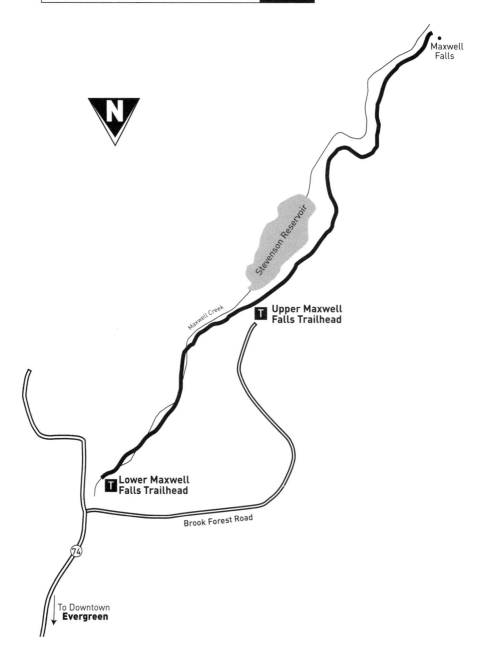

Wildlife: Deer, foxes, skunks, bears, coyotes, mountain lions, raccoons and a variety of birds and raptors.

Weather: Most of the trail is hidden in the trees, so wind, rain and sun are not factors. The trail is often snowy and slippery during the winter months, which makes it an ideal snowshoe trail after a big snow. The trail can be damp and mushy in the spring, so prepare to get muddy.

Other Users: Primarily hikers and mountain bikers.

Map: USGS 1:24,000 Map, Evergreen, Colorado, 1990.

Contact Info: Arapaho National Forest, Clear Creek Ranger District, (303) 567-3000; www.fs.fed.us/arnf/districts/ccrd/index.htm.

Mount Falcon Park (Morrison)
Run 28

Distance/Terrain: 6.0 to 11.0 miles (round-trip) on a variety of dirt and gravel singletrack trails.

Difficulty: Moderate to hard.

Elevation Change: Moderate to extreme.

Trailheads: The main trailhead is located just west of Colorado Highway 8 near the town of Morrison. (From Morrison, take Highway 74 west to Highway 8. Go about a mile south on Highway 8, and take a right on Forest Avenue. Go north on Vine Street and you'll run into the parking lot. Public restrooms are available at the main trailhead and the upper (west) trailhead.

Dogs: Dogs are allowed but must be on leash at all times.

Running Strollers: Nope. The trails are too steep, narrow and rocky.

Route Description: An early settler named John Brisben Walker once lived in an elaborate wood and stone house on Mount Falcon. Walker had visions of building the Summer White House, a vacation home for U.S. presidents. He laid the foundation but never got much further, because his original house burned to the ground in 1918.

Today Mount Falcon is one of the prized pieces of the Jefferson County Open Space system. It's a great place to run, but only if you don't mind steep climbs and congested trails. The trudge up the face of Mount Falcon is arduous and rocky, so be mentally prepared. The reward for your efforts are great views and a 4.0-mile downhill-all-the-way descent from the ruins of Walker's home.

Mount Falcon Park `Run 28`

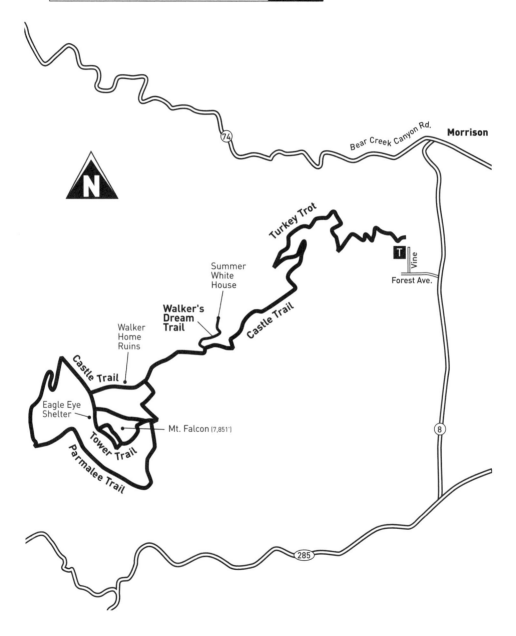

Starting from the parking lot, follow Turkey Trot Trail where it branches off to the right from Castle Trail. The 1.7-mile Turkey Trot is designed for foot travel only, whereas Castle Trail is open to mountain bikers and horseback riders. Turkey Trot is a fairly steep climb that runs counterclockwise around a small knob in the lower part of the park. The trail eventually connects with Castle Trail, but the grade is more moderate on the 1.2-mile climb to the junction with Two-Dog Trail and Walker's Dream Trail. (The foundation of the Summer White House is about 0.25 mile down Dream Trail.) As you continue on Castle Trail, the route gets flatter and wider while following a ridgeline that runs west past the ruins of Walker's home.

After about 3.0 miles of running, you'll come to an intersection with Meadow Trail, a short route to the Eagle Eye shelter atop Mount Falcon. Turn around and bomb down the same way you came for a 6.0-mile round-trip, but remember to take the Turkey Trot route near the bottom to avoid horse riders and mountain bikers.

Alternate Routes: To add more mileage, instead of turning around at the junction with Meadow Trail, continue to follow Castle Trail to the right for about 0.5 mile and pick up Parmalee Trail, a 2.0-mile section that loops around Mount Falcon. The backside offers occasional up-close views of majestic Mount Evans. It's occasionally steep, dropping and gaining about 850 feet before reconnecting with Meadow Trail about 0.5 mile from where you started the Parmalee loop. From there, you can follow Meadow Trail to the right and connect back to Castle Trail and continue down to the parking lot for a 10.5-mile run. Or you can zip up Tower Trail (at the end of Parmalee Trail) and crest Mount Falcon's 7,851-foot summit to take in 360-degree views of the Front Range (especially Mount Evans) before returning on Castle Trail for a 11.0-mile run.

Wildlife: Deer, foxes, skunks, bears, coyotes, mountain lions, raccoons and a variety of birds and raptors.

Weather: The trails on Mount Falcon are runnable year-round, but the north-facing slopes can be snowy and icy in the winter months. The lower trails are generally shielded from the wind, but the upper sections can be quite windy.

Other Users: Mountain bikers, hikers and equestrians.

Map: Mount Falcon Park Jefferson County Open Space, 2002.

Contact Info: (303) 271-5925, http://openspace.co.jefferson.co.us.

Morrison's Mount Falcon Park offers extraordinary views of Red Rocks Park and the Denver skyline.

Roxborough State Park (Littleton)
Run 29

Distance/Terrain: 2.5 to 12.0 miles on singletrack dirt trails.

Difficulty: Easy to Moderate. This park has several routes for all types of runners.

Elevation Change: Moderate. There are a few steep climbs, especially on the way up to Carpenter Peak.

Trailhead: To reach the park entrance, drive south on Wadsworth Boulevard (Highway 121) from C-470 about five miles until it curls to the left and ties in with Titan Road/Rampart Range Road. Take a right on that road and drive south to the park entrance about 3 miles ahead. All trails can be accessed from the visitor center parking lot, about 2 miles inside the park on Roxborough Drive. The park charges a $5 entry fee per vehicle. Public restrooms are available at the visitor center near the trailhead.

Dogs: Sorry Snoopy, no dogs allowed!

Running Strollers: No, not advised.

Route Description: Roxborough State Park has an assortment of short trails that can be linked to form runs up to 12.0 miles—or longer, if you connect to the Colorado Trail and/or nearby Waterton Canyon (see separate write-up below). As a warm-up, start with Fountain Valley Trail. The 2.5-mile loop begins north of the visitor center and winds through a variety of amazing red sandstone formations as it climbs slightly to Persse Place, a series of buildings built by early settler Henry S. Persse in 1900.

Once you return to the visitor center, you can link up with Willow Creek Loop (1.5 miles) or the South Rim Trail loop (3.0 miles) that stretch southward. The gentler of the two, Willow Creek Loop is known for abundant wildflowers in the summer. South Rim Trail is a narrow, moderately steep route that climbs high enough to offer spectacular views of the Fountain Valley loop you started on.

The gem of the park is Carpenter Peak Trail, a rugged 6.5-mile out-and-back trail that climbs to its namesake mountain in the western part of the park. The trail is accessed near the western Willow Creek/South Rim trail junction (about 0.5 mile south of the visitor center on Willow Creek Trail) and begins climbing immediately, gaining about 1,100 feet in 3.0 miles. It's a hearty run, but the magnificent views in all directions from the 7,200-foot peak make it well worth the effort.

Wildlife: Deer, coyotes, mountain lions, bobcats, squirrels, bears, foxes, elk, snakes and a variety of raptors.

Roxborough State Park

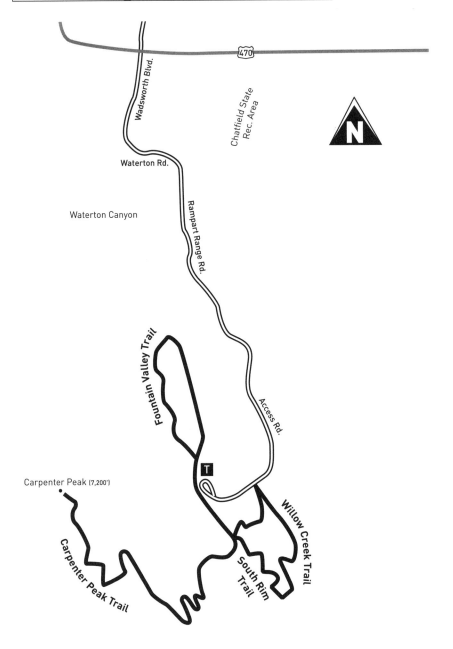

Weather: The park is open year-round, but some of the trails can hold snow and ice for a long time in winter. A few high points in the park can be windy, especially the upper reaches of Carpenter Peak.

Other Users: Hikers and bird-watchers. Mountain bikes and horses aren't allowed in the park.

Map: Roxborough State Park Map, Colorado State Parks.

Contact info: (303) 973-3959, www.parks.state.co.us/roxborough.

Waterton Canyon/ Colorado Trail (Littleton)
Run 30

Distance/Terrain: 12.5 miles (round-trip) on a flat unpaved road closed to motorized vehicles along the South Platte River.

Difficulty: Easy. The Colorado Trail section that connects at the upper end of the canyon is moderately challenging.

Elevation Change: Minimal to moderate. The dirt road rises about 340 feet in 6.0 miles from the trailhead to the Strontia Springs Dam. The Colorado Trail section beyond the dam is a rolling singletrack trail with a few short climbs.

Trailhead: The trailhead is located on Waterton Canyon Road, southwest of Chatfield State Park (see write-up in the "Other Trails" section that starts on page 130). From C-470, take Wadsworth Boulevard south about 5.0 miles, turn left on Waterton Road. The parking lot for Waterton Canyon and the Colorado Trail is located at the second left. Public restrooms are located at the trailhead.

Dogs: Dogs are permitted on a leash on the dirt road leading to Strontia Springs Dam, but they are not allowed on the adjacent trails in Waterton Canyon, primarily because it is a bighorn sheep habitat.

Running Strollers: Yes, the road from the trailhead to the dam can accommodate running strollers, but models built for trails work better than those designed for paved roads.

Route Description: Waterton Canyon and Strontia Springs Reservoir are owned by Denver Water, a governmental organization that oversees water service to the city and county of Denver and many of its surrounding suburbs. Midway through this run, you'll pass under a large water pipe that is pumping water to the metro area; you might wind up showering in some of it when you return home after your run. Denver Water and the U.S. Forest Service jointly maintain

Waterton Canyon/Colorado Trail Run 30

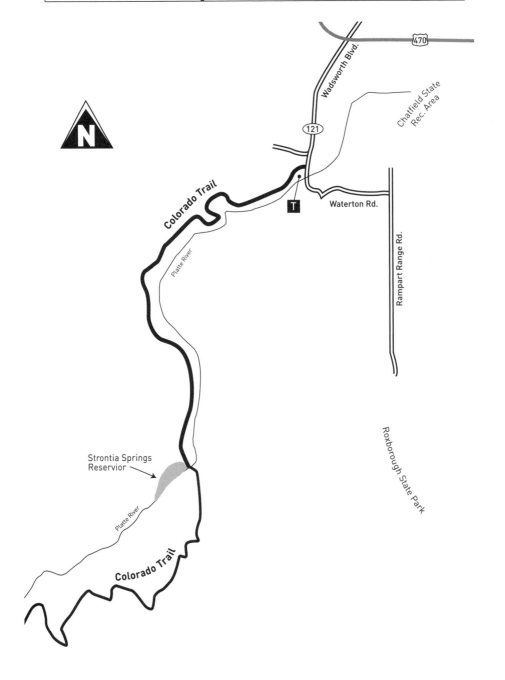

the trail and recreational facilities.

As scenic and peaceful as it is, this route is pretty basic. The dirt and gravel road twists and turns in stretches as it follows the meandering South Platte River below the dam. The farther you run, the higher the steep canyon walls become. But the elevation change is barely noticeable on the road until the very end, which is why it's a great place to run fast workouts or even a 12.5-mile out-and-back time trial. Near the end of the road, you'll see the impressive 243-foot-tall Strontia Springs Dam, which forms a reservoir that provides Denver with some of its drinking water.

Alternate Routes: Once at the dam, if you continue south for about 0.5 mile, the road ends and the trail branches into the undulating singletrack of the Colorado Trail (Trail 1776). From there, you can run all the way to Durango if your heart so desires, as this is a 487-mile trail that runs through the heart of Colorado's most rugged terrain. (You might make sure your feet desire it, too!) This was the route Boulder residents Buzz Burrell and Peter Bakwin took on their epic quest to set a Colorado trail running record in 1999. Although Bakwin was later sidelined with an injury after 330 miles, Burrell ran the entire route from Waterton Canyon to Durango in less than 12 days. Even if you don't run all the way to Durango, you can add mileage to your out-and-back run here or you can complete a 29-mile point-to-point run by continuing on this combination of epic singletrack and jeep road (Forest Road 538) through the community of South Platte and on to Buffalo Creek. Aside from arranging a ride at the other end, you'll need to carry sufficient water and perhaps extra clothing because that run will take you four to six hours or more.

Waterton Canyon also connects to the rugged trail system in Roxborough State Park (see write-up on page 121). If you take the steep, narrow trail that veers to the left just before the dam, you'll wind up connecting to the state park. If you can arrange a ride ahead of time, you can complete an 11-mile point-to-point run by taking the steeply descending Carpenter Peak trail to the visitor center.

Wildlife: Bighorn sheep (especially near the dam), deer, foxes, coyotes, bears, mountain lions and a variety of birds and raptors.
Weather: Waterton Canyon is open year-round, and the road is almost always runnable. Wind can be the biggest deterrent.
Other Users: Hikers, mountain bikers and anglers.
Maps: Waterton Canyon Map, Denver Water; BLM 1:100,000 Map, Bailey, Colorado.
Contact Info: (303) 628-6189 (Denver Water); (303) 275-5610 (Pike National Forest); www.water.denver.co.gov/recreation/strontia.html.

White Ranch Park (Golden)
Run 31

Distance/Terrain: 6.0 to 13.5 miles on singletrack rock and dirt trails.

Difficulty: Moderate to hard. There are a lot of hills and steep climbs throughout the park.

Elevation Change: Moderate to extreme. From the lower trailhead, you can expect 1,300 to 1,700 feet in elevation gain in about 4.5 miles, depending on your chosen route.

Trailheads: The lower trailhead (also known as the East Access) is located 1.0 mile west of Colorado Highway 93 on 56th Avenue, just north of Golden; to reach the upper trailhead (West Access), drive 4.1 miles west on Golden Gate Canyon Road to Crawford Gulch Road and follow signs to White Ranch Park.

Dogs: Yes, you can bring your pooches, but make sure they're always on a leash. And watch out for downhill mountain bikers and horseback riders, especially in tight terrain where dogs aren't easily visible.

Running Strollers: Not a chance. The trails are too steep and technical for strollers.

Route Description: Another gem in the Jefferson County Open Space system, White Ranch is chock full of steep singletrack trails, wildlife and pristine canyons, open meadows and forested foothills. It's a mix of intertwining trails, most of which are excellent for running. But it would be smart to take a map, because the rising, falling and constantly twisting trails make it easy to lose your bearings.

You'll probably want to start from the lower parking lot, if for no other reason than your run will end on a fun downhill and not a grueling climb. From the lower parking lot, Belcher Hill Trail starts to the north, but after crossing a small rocky prairie, it sneaks into a wooded grove around Van Bibbler Creek. After climbing a ridgeline and then dropping down to cross the creek about 1.0 mile into the run, you'll begin a long and arduous 3.0-mile climb to the summit of Belcher Hill on the west edge of the park. The trail climbs moderately to the north immediately after crossing the creek and then turns back to the southwest as it continues the ascent to the intersection with Longhorn Trail.

Stay on Belcher Hill Trail as it continues its undulating climb until you reach an intersection with Mustang Trail. Go left (west) on Mustang Trail, an undulating soft-dirt trail flanked by a variety of pine trees and steep canyon walls. When the trail turns to the north (roughly mile 3.0), it begins a steep climb up a lush, narrow canyon, eventually topping on Belcher Hill near a junction with Belcher Hill Trail. Make a left on Belcher Hill Trail, cross the paved park road, and begin a wild 0.5-

White Ranch Park Run 31

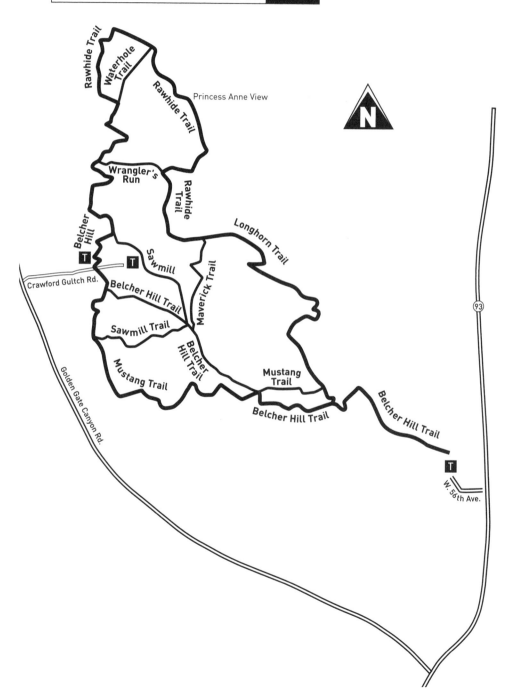

mile descent to the junction with Rawhide Trail (about mile 5.0).

Once on Rawhide Trail, you're in for a 2.0-mile up-and-down run to the north-west corner of the park. (If you want to shorten your run slightly, consider taking the Wrangler's Run cutoff midway through. It breaks off to the right after the next climb.) Rawhide Trail loops around the north end of the park, passing the Waterhole Trail cutoff twice in the process (mile 6.3, mile 7.2) and then begins an exciting 1.4-mile cruise along a steep, east-facing ridge. Rawhide Trail eventually gives way to Longhorn Trail (mile 9.0), a long, twisting downhill trail that eventually ties back into Belcher Trail (mile 11.8). From there, the trail flattens out. Cruise the final 1.7-mile singletrack back to the parking lot to complete an epic 13.5-mile route.

Wildlife: Deer, foxes, skunks, bears, coyotes, mountain lions, raccoons and a variety of birds and raptors.

Weather: The trails at White Ranch are runnable throughout the year, but the north-facing slopes can be snowy and icy in the winter months. Most of the trails are sheltered from the wind, although upper portions of Belcher Hill Trail, Mustang Trail and Rawhide Trail tend to be breezy.

Other Users: Mountain bikers, hikers, bird-watchers and equestrians.

Map: White Ranch Park, Jefferson County Open Space, 2002.

Contact Info: (303) 271-5975, http://openspace.co.jefferson.co.us

The Danielesque Trail Race at White Ranch Park in Golden is one of the best races along the Front Range.

Other Front Range West Trails

1. Alderfer/Three Sisters Park, Evergreen
Distance: Up to 12.5 miles. Difficulty: Easy to moderate. A 770-acre park in Evergreen, it's a great place for quiet runs on a mixture of soft forest trails and rocky singletrack trails. With 14 intertwining trails, it's hard to run the same route twice. One of the best is Evergreen Mountain Trail loop and Summit Trail extension on the south side of Buffalo Park Road, which offers spectacular views of Mount Evans from the top of Evergreen Mountain. Dogs are allowed but must be on leash at all times. For information, call (303) 271-5975 or go to http://openspace.co.jefferson.co.us.

2. Golden Gate Canyon State Park, Golden
Distance: 3.0 to 15.0 miles. Difficulty: Easy to hard. With a dozen well-marked, interconnecting trails, this 14,000-acre park is a perfect place for long, weekend runs. The best loops are the gently rolling 5.2-mile Mule Deer trail and the arduous 6.7-mile Mountain Lion route. There are plenty of ways to create your own loops, but don't start any run without a park map. A $5 vehicle fee is required to enter the park. Dogs must be on leash at all times. Call (303) 592-1502 or go to http://parks.state.co.us/golden_gate/.

3. Deer Creek Canyon Park, Littleton
Distance: Up to about 15.0 miles. Difficulty: Easy to moderate. This 1,881-acre park is the former campground site of Ute and Arapaho Indians. Seven linkable trails offer many options for trail runners. Although mountain bikes and horses are allowed at the park, there are three short trails totaling 2.6 miles for hikers and runners only. Dogs must be on leash at all times. For information, call (303) 271-5975 or go to http://openspace.co.jefferson.co.us

4. Chatfield State Park, Littleton
Distance: 4.0 to 20 miles. Difficulty: Easy. An expansive park on the southeast side of the Denver metro area, there are numerous loops to run without ever having to repeat the same section twice. A good place to start is near the horse corrals south of the Wadsworth Boulevard entrance on the west side of the park. Ultra-running guru Scott Weber typically hosts several trail races at the park every year (www.coachweber.com). He moved to South Carolina in 2003, but he was planning on continuing his race series. A $6 admission fee per vehicle is required to enter the park, unless you're running in a race. For information, call (303) 791-7275 or go to www.parks.state.co.us/chatfield.

5. Chimney Gulch and Lookout Mountain, Golden

Distance: 7.0 miles (round-trip). Difficulty: Moderate to hard. A steep trail that begins off Highway 6, this switch-backing route climbs to the top of Lookout Mountain. It can be a precarious run because of the steep drop-offs and arduous uphills (especially the first mile or so), but it's very rewarding nonetheless. The trail crosses Lookout Mountain Road several times and also includes a section for hikers and runners only. Upon reaching the Lookout Mountain Nature Center at the summit, you can turn around and complete a 7.0-mile round-trip or jog over to the top of Apex Park where more trails await. Dogs are allowed in Chimney Gulch, but not in the Lookout Mountain Nature Center. For information, call (303) 384-8100 or go to http://ci.golden.co.us/dept/parks/trails/trails.htm.

Front Range West
Running Resources

Track Facilities

There are several quality track surfaces in the foothills west of Denver, including both an indoor track and an outdoor facility at the Colorado School of Mines in Golden. But because the School of Mines is a private school, both are open only to faculty, staff, students and alumni. The indoor track in the CSM Steinhauer Fieldhouse is one of the best in the state, and CSM typically hosts two or three meets there every winter, occasionally accepting unattached runners with fast enough times to be competitive.

* Evergreen High School, 5300 S. Olive Rd., Evergreen
* Conifer High School, 10441 County Highway 73, Conifer
* Golden High School, 701 24th St., Golden
* Clear Creek High School, 320 Highway 103, Idaho Springs

Group Runs/Running Clubs

Colorado Masters Running Association typically holds several races and group runs for all ages and abilities throughout the year, including races in Waterton Canyon and Chatfield State Park. Call (303) 791-3384 for more details.

Evergreen Runners Circle, Evergreen, meets at 8:30 A.M. on Saturdays at various locations around Evergreen for 5- to 8-mile trail runs. Visit www.geocities.com/Colosseum/Lodge/7018/ or send an e-mail to rwesson@gld-mutt.cr.usgs.gov for more information.

Fastrek Running Club, Idaho Springs, meets for group runs and organizes rides to races. Call (303) 982-1958 for details of group runs and activities.

Rocky Mountain Road Runners, Denver/Front Range, typically meets at 8 A.M. on Sundays in the Waterton Canyon parking lot near South Platte Canyon Road and Kassler Road. The group also hosts a variety of races throughout the year, including a trail race in Waterton Canyon. Visit www.rmrr.org for more details.

Outdoor Sports Retailers

(Note: There isn't a specialty running retailer in the foothills west of Denver. However, some sports retailers, such as those listed below, carry running apparel and accessories like hydration packs, energy gels and maps.)

Foothills Ski and Bike
25948 Genesee Trail Rd. #J, Golden
(303) 526-2036

Maison de Ski
2804 Colorado Blvd., Idaho Springs
(303) 567-2044

Paragon Sports
2962 Evergreen Pkwy., Evergreen
(303) 670-0092

The Screaming Beagle Bike Shop
Evergreen Expressway and Squaw Pass, Evergreen
(303) 674-4418

Self-Propulsion
1212 Washington Ave., Golden
(303) 278-3290

Snow Leopard Mountain Sports
1240 Bergen Pkwy., A-100, Evergreen
(303) 674-2577
www.thesnowleopard.com

The Fort Collins Old Town Marathon and Half Marathon attracted about 1,200 runners in 2003.

Front Range North

Fort Collins, Greeley, Longmont, Loveland and Lyons

F ort Collins is without doubt one of the top running cities in the country. It has everything runners could ever want—a vibrant running community, several good running shops, a plethora of races from 5k to marathon and a gazillion great places to run.

Perhaps because it's a smaller city and located only an hour from high-profile Boulder, Fort Collins doesn't get much play in regional or national media. Although it's home to many elite racers—U.S. road running champion Libbie Hickman, American 1,500-meter ace Bryan Berryhill and masters standouts Jon Sinclair, Jane Welzel and Kim Jones, to name a few—it still tends to get little attention.

"There's a more competitive crowd in Boulder, I think, but there are a huge number of people in Fort Collins who are really into running," says Sinclair, one of the best road runners in U.S. history and a Fort Collins resident since 1975. "And there's a ton of places to run off-road."

Fort Collins is the hub of a strong running community in northern Colorado. With dozens of epic running trails in nearby Roosevelt National Forest, all-weather tracks in Fort Collins, Greeley and Loveland, countless road and trail races and several great running stores, it's no wonder locals don't want the word to get out. They want to keep it for themselves.

Carter Lake   Run 32

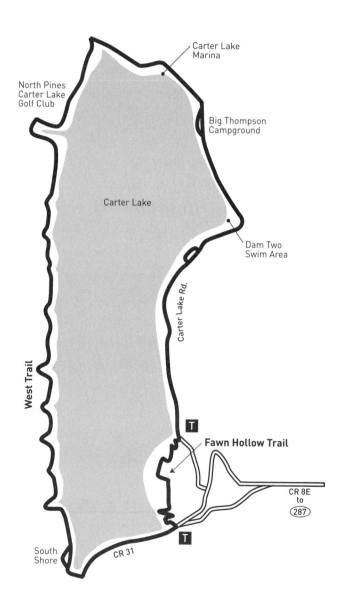

Carter Lake (Loveland)
Run 32

Distance/Terrain: 8.5 miles (round-trip) on singletrack dirt trails and paved roads.
Difficulty: Easy.
Elevation Change: Mild.
Trailheads: There are several places to park once inside the Carter Lake recreation area. To get to the park entrance, take County Road 8E west for about 4 miles from the southwest edge of Loveland. There is a $6 daily entrance fee per person. Restrooms are located inside the park.
Dogs: Dogs are allowed but must be leashed at all times and are restricted from the swim beach area.
Running Strollers: No.

Route Description: Carter Lake can be a relaxing place to get in a good run, so long as you don't mind the buzz of motorboats pulling water-skiers on the lake. The 8.5-mile loop is mostly flat and as fast as you want it to be. Starting from the South Shore parking area, start your run in a counterclockwise direction on County Road 31. When you get to the southeast corner of the lake, take the shortcut on Fawn Hollow Trail. You'll pop back out on the busy road after 0.5 mile, so keep your eyes peeled for oncoming traffic. Run on the road along the lake's eastern shore, passing Carter Knolls, Dam Two Swim Area and the Big Thompson Campground. As you reach the north end of the lake, you'll pass the Carter Lake Marina and Lowell and Eagle campgrounds. Keep running: The best is yet to come. After passing the North Pines area (and the Carter Lake Sail Club), follow the sign to West Trail. From here it's a delightful 3.2 miles back to where you started on a singletrack route hugging the lake's west bank.

Wildlife: Deer, coyotes, foxes, squirrels, raccoons and a variety of birds and raptors.
Weather: The road on the lake's east side can be prone to high winds.
Other Users: Hikers, mountain bikers and boat users.
Map: Carter Lake Map, Larimer County Parks & Open Lands Department.
Contact Info: (970) 498-1100, www.co.larimer.co.us/parks/carter.htm.

Hall Ranch Run 33

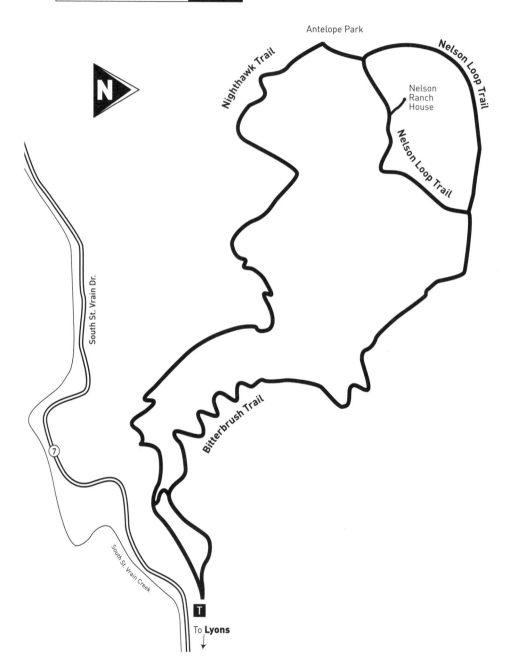

Antelope Park

Nelson Loop Trail

Nighthawk Trail

Nelson
Ranch
House

Nelson Loop Trail

South St. Vrain Dr.

Bitterbrush Trail

South St. Vrain Creek

7

T

To **Lyons**

Hall Ranch (Lyons)
Run 33

Distance/Terrain: 9.5 miles (round-trip), primarily on singletrack dirt trails.

Difficulty: Moderate.

Elevation Change: Moderate. The trail has a few steep climbs, but it also has plenty of mild rolling sections and fun downhills.

Trailheads: The park entrance and main trailhead, located on Colorado Highway 7, is 1 mile west of Lyons. Restrooms are available at the trailhead.

Dogs: Dogs are not allowed at Hall Ranch, because it is considered wildlife habitat.

Running Strollers: Nope.

Route Description: Arapaho and Cheyenne Indians once occupied the 3,206 acres that make up Hall Ranch Open Space. Since the late 1900s, the land has been prospected, farmed and quarried for sandstone. Many of the buildings on the University of Colorado's Boulder campus were built using stone from quarries that once dotted this property.

Hall Ranch, a Boulder County Open Space park, is home to a spectacular 9.5-mile singletrack circuit on the Bitterbrush, Nelson Loop and Nighthawk trails. From the trailhead west of Lyons on Highway 7, run up the 4.7-mile no-bikes-allowed Nighthawk Trail to Antelope Park. It's a steady climb on a technical trail, but it's not as steep as the beginning of the Bitterbrush Trail. At the top of the Nighthawk Trail, you'll reach a fork in the trail in an area called Antelope Park. Veer right and take the short connector trail to reach Nelson Loop. Go right on Nelson Loop's 1.1-mile southeast flank down to the 3.7-mile rolling descent of Bitterbrush. Before you reach Bitterbrush Trail again be sure to take a peek at the historic Nelson Ranch house (in the middle of Nelson Loop) and Longs Peak on the western horizon. Your return to the parking lot on Bitterbrush Trail is open, scenic and mostly downhill (except for a few slight inclines). But make sure you keep your eyes and ears open for oncoming mountain bikers and horseback riders. The final 1.5 miles is filled with technical switchbacks, so watch your footing.

Wildlife: Golden eagles, great horned owls, hawks, mountain lions, elk, bighorn sheep, white-tailed deer, black-tailed prairie dogs, coyotes, foxes, badgers, bobcats and prairie rattlesnakes.

Weather: The trail is accessible year-round, but it is prone to snow in the winter months and high winds throughout the year.

Other Users: Mountain bikers, horseback riders and hikers. (This is one of the more popular mountain bike trails north of Denver, so keep your eyes peeled at all times!)

Maps: Hall Ranch Open Space Map, Boulder County Parks & Open Space Dept.

Contact Info: (303) 441-3950, www.co.boulder.co.us/openspace.

Horsetooth Mountain Park
(Fort Collins)
Run 34

Distance/Terrain: 3.0 to 13.0 miles or more (round-trip), primarily on singletrack dirt trails.

Difficulty: Easy to hard.

Elevation Change: Moderate to extreme. One of the steepest trails is the route up Horsetooth Rock, which climbs 1,700 feet in about 3.5 miles.

Trailheads: The park entrance is on the north side of County Road 38E, just west of Horsetooth Reservoir. From South Taft Hill Road on the west side of Fort Collins, take County Road 38E about 6.3 miles as it winds around the south end of Horsetooth Reservoir. There is a $6 daily fee per person, even if you enter on foot. Restrooms are available at the main trailhead.

Dogs: Dogs are allowed but must be leashed at all times.

Running Strollers: Not advised.

Route Description: What kind of running mood are you in? Do you want to run smooth, rolling trails at a fast pace? Do you want to do some classic climbing or hill repeats? Horsetooth Mountain Park has 28 miles of trails that cover the gamut of possibilities. Regardless of your route, you're likely to encounter wildflower meadows (in late spring and summer), aspen groves, thick conifer forests, reddish "hogback" rock outcroppings, precipices, high canyon walls and breathtaking vistas.

For a moderate 9.5-mile loop with plenty of hills, start from the park entrance and take Horsetooth Falls Trail to the sometimes gushing, sometimes trickling waterfall of Spring Creek. The falls, less than a mile from the trailhead, are in a gorge encased by high cliff walls. After seeing the falls, continue on the trail you were on and climb a series of moderately steep switchbacks (mile 1.5). You can get another good view of the falls from several hundred feet above, as well as a nice glimpse of Horsetooth Reservoir and Fort Collins below.

You'll come to a three-way fork in the trail with Soderberg Trail and Spring Creek Trail. Follow Spring Creek Trail to the (north), passing straight through the

Horsetooth Mountain Park Run 34

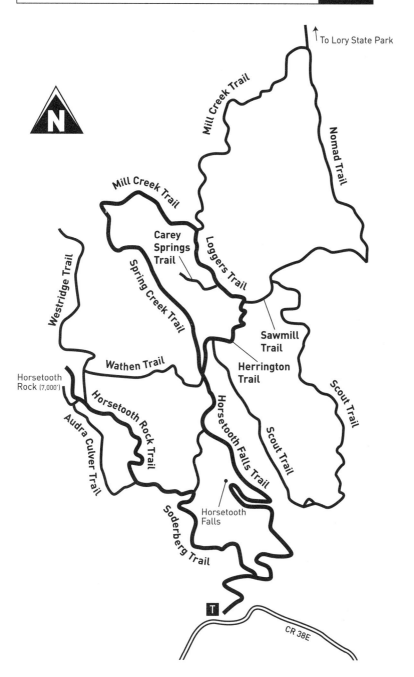

To Lory State Park

Mill Creek Trail

Nomad Trail

Mill Creek Trail

Carey Springs Trail

Loggers Trail

Westridge Trail

Spring Creek Trail

Sawmill Trail

Herrington Trail

Wathen Trail

Scout Trail

Horsetooth Rock (7,000')

Horsetooth Rock Trail

Audra Culver Trail

Horsetooth Falls Trail

Scout Trail

Horsetooth Falls

Soderberg Trail

T

CR 38E

Horsetooth Falls is one of the many attractions you see on a run in Horsetooth Mountain Park.

Wathen/Herrington trail junction and continue as it winds along its namesake creek and climbs about 1,000 feet in the span of about 3.0 miles. The trail eventually parts from Spring Creek, climbs a high ridge (mile 4.5) and then begins a fun descent into the Mill Creek drainage. At a three-way junction (mile 6.0) with Mill Creek Trail and Loggers Trail, take a right on Loggers Trail and wind your way back to the park entrance via Herrington, Spring Creek and Soderberg trails. There are almost as many twists and turns on the way back as you encountered on the way in, so the final 1.5-mile downhill portion of Soderberg Trail is a welcome relief.

Alternate Routes: There are seemingly limitless routes that can be made by connecting the park's various trails. For a very difficult 7.5-mile loop with a major climb, consider running on Horsetooth Rock Trail to the top of the park's distinctive namesake peak (7,260 feet) and returning via Wathen, Spring Creek and Soderberg trails. For a relatively easy 3.0-mile loop, connect the Soderberg, Spring Creek and Horsetooth Falls trails.

The only similarity between any two runs is that each one must start and end at the park entrance. Unless, of course, you decide to do a 9.0-mile point-to-point run that connects with the trails inside Lory State Park. But for that you'll need to stash a car or have a friend pick you up at the other end.

Wildlife: Mule deer, coyotes, raccoons, striped skunks, squirrels, cottontail rabbits, porcupines and red foxes.

Weather: Some of the park's trails can be windy, but most are protected. Winter and spring mean snowy and muddy trails.

Other Users: Hikers, mountain bikers and horseback riders.

Maps: Horsetooth Mountain Park Map, Larimer County Parks & Open Lands Department.

Contact Info: (970) 679-4570, www.co.larimer.co.us/parks/htmp.htm.

Longs Peak Trail `Run 35`

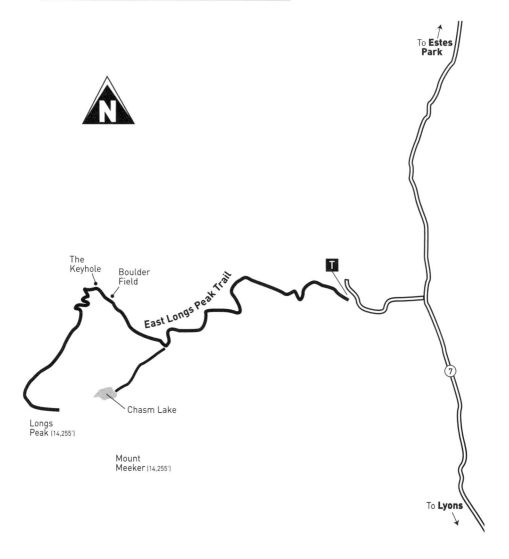

To **Estes Park**

N

The Keyhole

Boulder Field

East Longs Peak Trail

T

Chasm Lake

Longs Peak (14,255')

Mount Meeker (14,255')

7

To **Lyons**

Longs Peak Trail
(Rocky Mountain National Park)
Run 35

Distance/Terrain: Up to 15.0 miles (round-trip) on rugged singletrack trails.
Difficulty: Hard.
Elevation Change: Moderate to extreme.
Trailhead: The Longs Peak trailhead is located along Colorado Highway 7 about 10 miles south of Estes Park. There is a restroom at the trailhead, but no food and beverage concessionaire.
Dogs: Dogs are not allowed.
Running Strollers: No.

Route Description: One of the most challenging but satisfying trails along the Front Range, Longs Peak Trail can be devilishly grueling and leave you gasping for air—even if you opt only for the 8.5-mile round-trip to Chasm Lake.

From the parking lot at about 9,500 feet, Longs Peak Trail climbs briskly through a heavily wooded area, crossing several streams and waterfalls along the way. The grade varies in the forest, but then levels out briefly once the trail gets above tree line. The trail is rocky and footing is dicey the entire way, especially the first mile or so above tree line. After about 3.5 miles of uphill running, you'll come to a fork in the trail. Take a left and enjoy a gentle 0.75-mile descent to Chasm Lake and Columbine Falls; it will make the difficult climb up from the parking lot well worth your efforts. After soaking in the scene below Longs Peak's vaunted East Face, turn around and enjoy the views of the eastern plains on the way down. But be sure to watch your step on the rocky trail!

Alternate Routes: For hearty runners who want a mightier challenge, go right at Chasm Lake on East Longs Peak Trail and head for the 14,255-foot summit. (Check with the rangers ahead of time to make sure the trail is open; typically the snow doesn't make the trail passable with running shoes until late June or early July.) While this is a difficult trail, it's easier to run the section between 12,000 and 13,000 feet than some of the lower sections. But your gait will likely slow considerably when you get to the mile-long boulder field below the famed Keyhole (13,150 feet). If you can make it that far, continue on for the final 1.5 miles around the back side of the mountain and up to the summit. There is no more running left to be done once you reach the Keyhole; from there it's hiking and Class 2, 3 and 4 scrambling. Even so, a strong runner should be able to complete this 15.0-mile round-trip in less than 4.5 hours.

If you want to run to the summit of Longs Peak, be smart and plan ahead. You must carry a hydration pack with at least 40 ounces of water, as well as an extra layer of clothing and snack food. Your body will dehydrate quicker at high altitude, so be sure to drink water early and often. Weather conditions can change in a matter of minutes at high altitudes, regardless of how sunny the sky might be. Be sure to start early to avoid the thunderstorms that occur on most afternoons during summer. Running this trail alone is not advised.

Wildlife: Deer, foxes, raccoons, marmots and a variety of birds and raptors.
Weather: Longs Peak Trail is accessible year-round, but it's runnable only from May until early October. It is a splendid snowshoe trail in the winter months, but even more challenging than it is in the summer. The trail is susceptible to high winds.
Other Users: Hikers and campers.
Maps: Rocky Mountain National Park Visitor Map, National Park Service.
Contact Info: (970) 586-1206, www.nps.gov/romo.

Lory State Park (Fort Collins)
Run 36

Distance/Terrain: About 7.3 miles (round-trip) on singletrack trails, ranging from soft flat paths to steep, rocky routes.
Difficulty: Easy to hard.
Elevation Change: Moderate to extreme. The 1.8-mile ascent up Arthur's Rock Trail climbs about 1,500 feet.
Trailhead: Park at the Lory State Park Visitor Center at the north end of the park. The trailhead is located about 5 miles due west of Fort Collins on the west side of Horsetooth Reservoir, but it takes about 12 miles of driving to get there. Take U.S. 287 north from Fort Collins through LaPorte, turn left at the Bellvue exit onto County Road 23N. Turn left again, go 1.4 miles and take a right on County Road 25G. Drive another 1.6 miles to the park entrance. There is a $5 daily entry fee per vehicle. Restrooms are available at the visitor center.
Dogs: Dogs are allowed but must be on leash at all times.
Running Strollers: No, unless you're running on the park roads—which would be silly—you're not going to find trails smooth enough to handle strollers.

Lory State Park Run 36

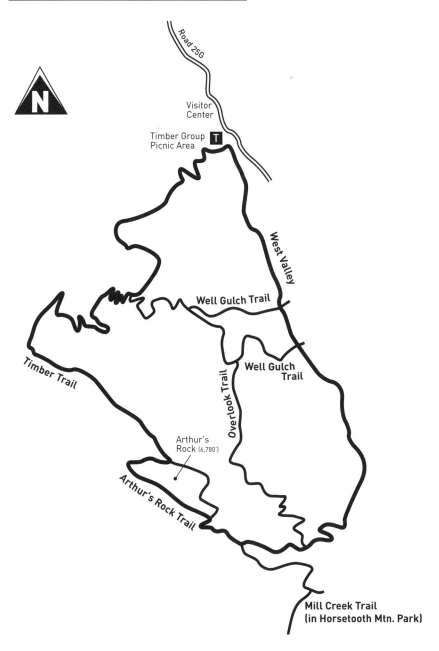

Road 25G

Visitor
Center

Timber Group
Picnic Area **T**

West Valley

Well Gulch Trail

Timber Trail

Overlook Trail

Well Gulch
Trail

Arthur's
Rock (6,780')

Arthur's Rock Trail

Mill Creek Trail
(in Horsetooth Mtn. Park)

Route Description: This state park offers something for whatever kind of mood you're in, but the best trails involve some serious uphill running. The payoff is sensational views of Horsetooth Reservoir and Fort Collins, as well as the flat-lands of northeastern Colorado.

Starting from the Timber Group Picnic Area parking lot just inside the park, start your run on the mostly flat West Valley Trail as it parallels the park road that winds southward. This is an excellent way to warm up your legs for the steep climbs that are to come. You'll pass several parking areas and cross Well Gulch Trail twice. After about 2.0 miles, West Valley Trail intersects with Arthur's Rock Trail near a parking lot at the end of the road. Head west on Arthur's Rock Trail as it begins a gradual climb up Arthur's Rock Gulch. The views and waterfall activity increase the farther you run, but so does the incline.

After about 1.0 mile, you'll reach a fork in the trail. Continue on either branch, as each will lead you to the 6,780-foot summit of the trail near the massive Arthur's Rock. Chances are you'll need a breather after climbing 1,500 feet in about 1.8 miles, so stop and take in the incredible views of the valley below. When your heart rate has dropped down to a reasonable level, continue running on the Timber Trail, which will take you 3.5 miles back to where you started.

The aptly named Timber Trail veers through classic Colorado forest, lush with both ponderosa pine and Douglas fir. After about 1.0 mile of meandering, the trail begins a steep descent on a series of switchbacks down into Well Gulch. Bypass Well Gulch Trail and continue as Timber Trail descends more gently for the remaining 1.75 miles to the parking area.

Alternate Routes: Two other trails are worth checking out: The 1.5-mile Well Gulch Trail connects the West Valley and Timber trails via a moderate climb and descent; the 1.9-mile Overlook Trail runs between Well Gulch Trail and Arthur's Rock Trail. Also, instead of running up Arthur's Rock Trail, you can stay on West Valley Trail, which will eventually lead you to Horsetooth Mountain, making numerous longer runs possible.

Wildlife: Mule deer, coyotes, raccoons, striped skunks, squirrels, cottontail rabbits, porcupines and red foxes are common; black bears, mountain lions, bobcats, elk, bighorn sheep can be seen occasionally.

Weather: The park is open year-round, but some of the upper trails can be icy, snowy and muddy during winter and muddy during spring.

Other Users: Hikers (on all trails), mountain bikers and equestrians (on select trails only).

Maps: Lory State Park Trails Map, Colorado State Parks.

Contact Info: (970) 493-1623, www.parks.state.co.us.

A steep climb to Arthurs' Rock awaits runners at Lory State Park in Fort Collins.

Old Flowers Road Run 37

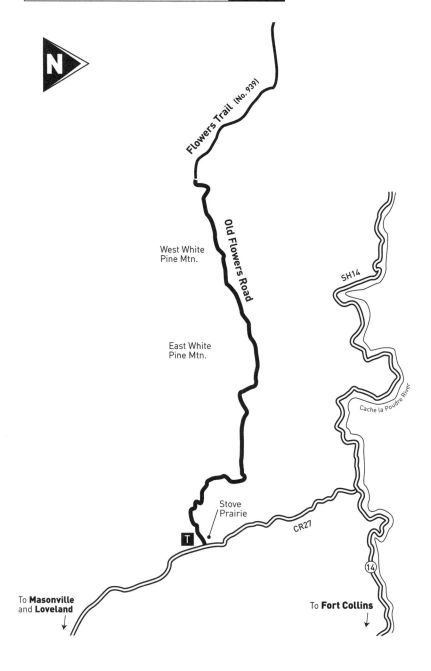

N

Flowers Trail (No. 939)

Old Flowers Road

West White
Pine Mtn.

East White
Pine Mtn.

SH14

Cache la Poudre River

Stove
Prairie

T

CR27

14

To **Masonville**
and **Loveland**

To **Fort Collins**

Old Flowers Road
(West of Fort Collins)
Run 37

Distance/Terrain: Up to 30 miles (round-trip) on a dirt and gravel fire road.
Difficulty: Moderate to hard.
Elevation Change: Moderate. Although the road climbs about 2,000 feet in 10 miles, most of the climbs are gradual.
Trailheads: There is no trailhead, but most runners park near an area called Stove Prairie. To reach the area, take Colorado 14 west of Fort Collins, turn left on County Road 27 and go south for about 4 miles to the intersection with County Road 52E. Old Flowers Road (or simply Flowers Road, as it is called by some) starts out as Country Road 52E but turns into Forest Service Road 152.
Dogs: Yes, dogs are allowed, but technically you need to keep Fido on a leash, because the road and trail are under U.S. Forest Service jurisdiction.
Running Strollers: Not advised.

Route Description: This rugged mountain road west of Fort Collins sees very little vehicular traffic, which makes it a popular place for mountain bikers, marathoners and ultrarunners from northern Colorado. It's an ideal place to log high-altitude mountain runs (6,000 to 9,000 feet) of three to four hours. The road climbs as it heads west and has plenty of rolling hills in the Cache la Poudre Wilderness Area. The road passes to the north of the twin 10,000-foot peaks of West and East White Pine mountains and eventually crosses the South Fork of the Cache la Poudre. About 15 miles from the parking area near Stove Prairie, the road ends at an elevation of about 8,900 feet and turns into Flowers Trail (Trail 939), which follows Beaver Creek into the Comanche Peak Wilderness Area. With many connecting trails and mountain roads, you can run as long as you want on Flowers Road and Flowers Trail. But, like all mountain runs, it's wise to take a map, plenty of water, an extra layer of clothing, some snacks and, if possible, a running partner.

Wildlife: You name it—deer, foxes, coyotes, black bears, mountain lions, skunks, raccoons, elk, owls, hawks and rattlesnakes.
Weather: The road is closed in winter because of heavy snows and drifting.
Other Users: Mountain bikers and an occasional four-wheel-drive vehicle.
Maps: USGS 1:24,000 Maps Buckhorn Mountain, Crystal Mountain, Pingree Park, Chambers Lake and Comanche Peak.
Contact Info: (970) 498-1100, www.fs.fed.us/r2/arnf.

Pawnee Buttes Run 38

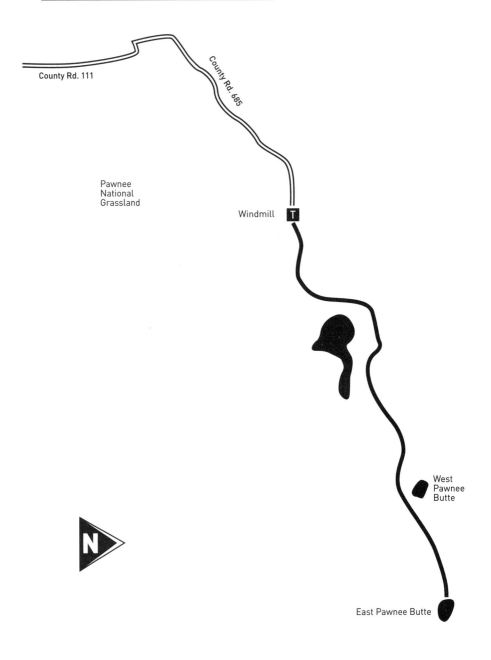

County Rd. 111

County Rd. 685

Pawnee
National
Grassland

Windmill **T**

West
Pawnee
Butte

East Pawnee Butte

N

Pawnee Buttes (Keota)
Run 38

Distance/Terrain: 4.2 miles (round-trip) on dirt and gravel trails and jeep roads.
Difficulty: Easy.
Elevation Change: Minimal; climbs about 240 feet in two miles.
Trailheads: The trailhead is located about 40 miles northwest of Greeley. To get there, take Colorado Highway 14 to the Keota exit. From the near-extinct town of Keota, follow County Road 105 north for about 3 miles, take a right on County Road 104 and drive 3 miles east to County Road 111. Go north on 111 for almost 5 miles, turning off on Road 685. Continue down the road to the trailhead near a large wooden windmill, one of many ancient wind-powered water pumps that dot the area.
Dogs: Dogs are allowed but must be on leash at all times.
Running Strollers: No, they won't work very well on this trail.

Route Description: You might think it hard to justify driving such a long way for such a short run, but Pawnee Buttes is unique and definitely worth the trip. The area features a spectacular collection of pink and brown rock formations—the most notable being the massive West Butte and East Butte—believed to date back 70 million to 90 million years. The eroded sandstone buttes were created by a series of ancient rivers and streams. As a result, the once-lush area is abundant with fossil material from previous eras. Fossils from ancient horses, turtles, vultures and camels have been found here. (It is illegal to take any fossils or artifacts from this U.S. Forest Service area.)

Pawnee Buttes Trail is rocky in places as it meanders to the East Butte, just technical enough to slow you down a bit. The route twists and turns in the first 0.25 mile, descending to a small prairie. From there, it crosses a draw, passes through an old barbed-wire fence and descends slightly to a grassy plain. A long, gradual ascent through pristine grassland leads to a gravel road near West Butte. A short jaunt farther down the jeep road dead-ends near the base of East Butte.

The views are much different than those offered along most foothill trails. Instead of providing vistas of heavy timber, rugged mountains or urban sprawl, a run on Pawnee Buttes Trail offers a glimpse of Colorado's other half—the barren eastern plains. In the spring and early summer, yucca, juniper, prickly pear and a variety of low-lying wildflowers are mixed in with the native grasses that somehow find enough moisture to thrive in the arid climate.

Running this short out-and-back run might seem unremarkable the first time out, but if you have time, do it twice. You'll notice and appreciate it much more on the second go-round. When you're done, rent the video version of James Michener's *Centennial* and you'll want to return again and again. This is definitely a run where you should carry water, especially in the hot, dry summer months. Otherwise, some paleontologist might dig up a fossilized runner in a few hundred years.

Wildlife: Hawks, falcons, coyotes, pronghorn antelope and deer mice.
Weather: The trail is open year-round. Wind and exposure to the sun are the only
    detractors as far as weather goes.
Other Users: Hikers and bird watchers. Mountain bikes are not allowed on this trail.
Maps: Pawnee Buttes Area map, U.S. Forest Service.
Contact Info: (970) 353-5004, www.fs.fed.us/arnf/districts/png/hiking.

Poudre River Trail (East)
(Windsor/Greeley)
Run 39

Distance/Terrain: Up to 14.0 miles (round-trip), depending on where you start, on
    wide concrete paths.
Difficulty: Easy.
Elevation Change: Minimal. The trail is generally flat, except for a few gentle slopes.
Trailheads: There are several access points to Poudre River Trail, including Island
    Grove Regional Park and Poudre River Ranch, the site for the yet-to-be-built
    Poudre Learning Center on 83rd Avenue in Greeley, Eastman Park in Windsor
    and a trailhead on Country Road 62 near the Kodak plant in east Windsor. There
    are no restrooms at any of the trailheads.
Dogs: Yes, but your mutt needs to be on a leash.
Running Strollers: Yes, the trail is perfect for strollers.

Route Description: When completed, Poudre River Trail will be a 19-mile concrete path from Island Grove Regional Park in Greeley to the Weld-Larimer county line along the meandering Cache la Poudre River. Long-range plans call for the trail to connect with Fort Collins' Poudre Trail (see the write-up on page 156). The trail is being built through a cooperative effort between the cities of Greeley and Windsor and Weld County.

Poudre River Trail (East) `Run 39`

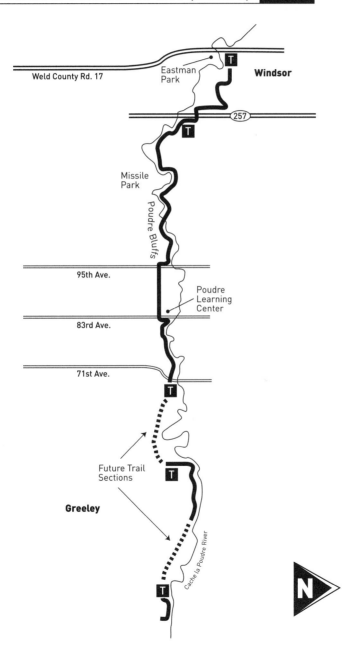

Weld County Rd. 17

Eastman Park

Windsor

257

Missile Park

Poudre Bluffs

95th Ave.

Poudre Learning Center

83rd Ave.

71st Ave.

Future Trail Sections

Greeley

Cache la Poudre River

N

As of spring 2003, about 8 miles of trail were completed in three separate sections. The longest continuous section of trail stretches 7.0 miles from the eastern terminus at Eastman Park in Windsor to 71st Avenue in Greeley. The trail, which has a few road crossings, is ideal for slow leisurely runs or fast-paced workouts. It passes through residential, agricultural and industrial portions of Greeley, Windsor and Weld County, offering a glimpse of both the past and present significance of the Poudre River. The areas surrounding the trail and the river have abundant wildlife and sites of historical interest, including a World War II U.S. Army German prisoner-of-war camp, the former Sharktooth ski area (which operated on an adjacent bluff in the early 1970s) and a series of Cold War missile silos. Poudre River Trail is the site of a few races, including a 5k and a duathlon.

Wildlife: Deer, foxes, skunks, mink, raccoons, coyotes, frogs, turtles, snakes and many varieties of birds can be seen along the river trail.

Weather: Although open year-round and generally protected from foul weather, the trail is not maintained during the winter, when certain sections can be prone to drifting snow.

Other Users: Bicyclists, walkers and inline skaters.

Map: Poudre River Trail Map, Poudre River Trail Corridor Inc.

Contact Info: (970) 350-9783, www.poudretrail.org.

Poudre River Trail (West)
(Fort Collins)
Run 40

Distance/Terrain: Up to 16.6 miles (round-trip), depending on starting point, on wide concrete bike paths.

Difficulty: Easy.

Elevation Change: Minimal.

Trailhead: There are dozens of places to pick up the trail, including Lee Martinez Park and Natural Area, Buckingham Park, Kingfisher Point Natural Area and a trailhead on North Taft Hill Road. Only a few of the trail access points have restrooms, but there are many restaurants and public buildings within close proximity to the route.

Dogs: Dogs are allowed on the trail, but must be on a leash at all times.

Running Strollers: Yes, this is one of the longest stroller-accessible routes on the Front Range.

Poudre River Trail (West) Run 40

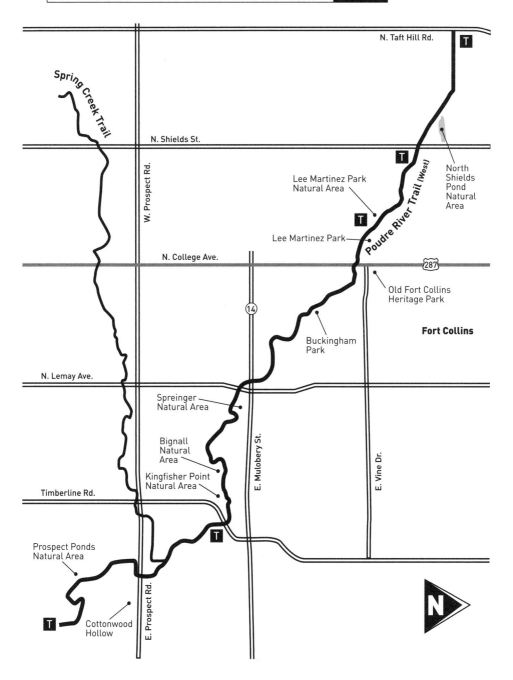

N. Taft Hill Rd.

Spring Creek Trail

N. Shields St.

W. Prospect Rd.

Poudre River Trail (West)

North Shields Pond Natural Area

Lee Martinez Park Natural Area

Lee Martinez Park

N. College Ave.

287

Old Fort Collins Heritage Park

Fort Collins

14

Buckingham Park

N. Lemay Ave.

Spreinger Natural Area

Bignall Natural Area

Kingfisher Point Natural Area

E. Mulobery St.

E. Vine Dr.

Timberline Rd.

Prospect Ponds Natural Area

E. Prospect Rd.

Cottonwood Hollow

N

Route Description: Three cheers for cities that have developed urban trails that minimize road crossings. Fort Collins has two such trails, each of which is an ideal place to run just about any kind of workout. Poudre River Trail starts in the northwest corner of Fort Collins' city limits on North Taft Hill Road and runs in a southeasterly direction to the Environmental Learning Center on East Drake Road. (Long-range plans call for the trail to be extended west to the town of LaPorte and east to the Arapahoe Bend Natural Area, where it might eventually pass under I-25 and connect with the Poudre River Trail between Windsor and Greeley.) The trail follows the quietly bubbling Cache la Poudre River and passes numerous wildlife-rich natural areas and through Lee Martinez Park north of downtown. Along its 8.3-mile journey through the city, the twisting trail passes under a 100-year-old railroad bridge, an old pickle factory and residential areas.

The Fort Collins Old Town Marathon and Half-Marathon run along a long portion of the Poudre River Trail in early May (www.runnersroostftcollins.com).

Alternate Routes: The trail connects with the 10.0-mile Spring Creek bike path (see "Other Northern Front Range Trails" on page 162) just east of the intersection of Timberline and Prospect roads, making it relatively easy to do long out-and-back training runs of 15 to 30 miles almost completely devoid of road crossings.

Wildlife: Deer, foxes, raccoons, skunks, squirrels, frogs, turtles, snakes and a variety of birds.

Weather: The trail is accessible 365 days a year. Although not maintained in winter, buildings, trees and geographical features keep it well protected from wind.

Other Users: Bicyclists, walkers and inline skaters.

Map: Fort Collins Bike Map, City of Fort Collins.

Contact info: (970) 224-6126, www.fcgov.com/parks/trails.php.

The scenic and serene Poudre River Trail through Fort Collins is an ideal getaway for short or long runs.

Round Mountain National Recreation Trail
(West of Loveland)
Run 41

Distance/Terrain: 9.2 miles (round trip) on singletrack dirt/rock trails.

Difficulty: Moderate to hard.

Elevation Change: Moderate to extreme. The trail climbs about 3,000 feet in 4.6 miles to the summit.

Trailheads: The trailhead is located on U.S. Highway 34, about 10 miles west of Loveland. There is a restroom at the trailhead.

Dogs: Dogs are allowed but must be on leash at all times.

Running Strollers: Nope. Don't even think about it.

Route Description: So you want to some good hill work, huh? Head to Round Mountain National Recreation Trail and you'll get plenty of vertical gain in a relatively short run. Even though it starts at a relatively low elevation (about 5,800 feet), you're going to be huffin' and puffin' at the start of this one. The trail climbs furiously out of the Big Thompson River Valley, although not too steep to stop you from running. After a steep 1.0 mile, the grade becomes slightly more gradual and starts to get more scenic, but the footing of the trail also gets more rocky for about 1.5 miles. Once out of the rocks, the trail passes through a lush ravine and more conifer groves and eventually reaches the 8,450-foot summit. From the top, you can see Longs Peak to the west, Carter Lake to the south and the city of Loveland to the east.

Wildlife: Deer, black bears, mountain lions, elk, raccoons, foxes, skunks, rattlesnakes and a variety of birds and raptors.

Weather: Because of its relatively low elevation, this mountain trail is accessible most of the year. Still, it is usually snowy and icy for a few weeks after a big snow, and it can be quite muddy in winter and spring.

Other Users: Mountain bikers and horseback riders.

Map: USGS 1:24,000 Map, Drake, Colorado, 1984.

Contact Info: (970) 498-1100, www.fs.fed.us/r2/arnf.

Round Mountain National Recreation Trail
Run 41

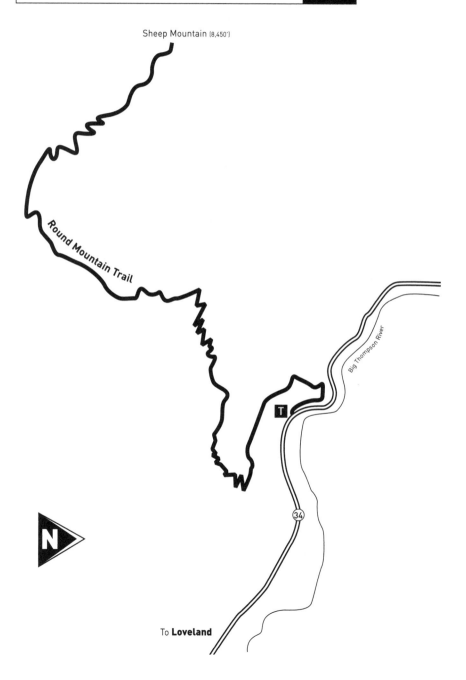

Sheep Mountain (8,450')

Round Mountain Trail

Big Thompson River

T

34

N

To **Loveland**

Other Front Range North Trails

1. Spring Creek Trail, Fort Collins

Distance: Up to 10.0 miles (one way). Difficulty: Easy. The concrete bike path of Spring Creek Trail follows its namesake creek through central Fort Collins from West Drake Road to the confluence of Spring Creek and the Cache la Poudre River on the east side of the city. Although an extremely popular route and often crowded on weekends and summer evenings, it's convenient and generally flat. Dogs are allowed but must be leashed at all times. (970) 224-6126, www.fcgov.com/parks/trails.php.

2. St. Vrain Greenway, Longmont

Distance: 6.4 miles (one way). Difficulty: Easy. This 3.2-mile concrete path follows the St. Vrain River as it winds its way through Longmont. There are several places to pick up the trail, but the best starting points are the western terminus at the Golden Ponds Nature Area west of Hover Road, or the eastern terminus in the parking lot north of Woody's Wood-fired Pizza on Main Street. Either way, it's a mostly flat route perfect for early morning runs or up-tempo workouts (there are no road crossings). Dogs are allowed but must be on a leash. Look for the Tabernash/Left Hand Canyon Brewing Company on the north side of the trail midway through the route, but try to stay out of the tasting room until after you've finished your run. (303) 776-6050, www.ci.longmont.co.us.

3. Recreation Trail, Loveland

Distance: 13 miles (one way). Difficulty: Easy. This is actually a two-part paved trail that starts at the Chilson Recreation Center on the east side of town. The western section follows the Big Thompson River for about 6.0 miles from Wilson Road to Colorado Highway 287. The eastern/northern section starts at the rec center and follows Loveland and Greeley Canal north about 7.0 miles to Boyd Lake State Park. (970) 962-2727, www.ci.loveland.co.us/parksrec/rectrails.htm.

4. Devil's Backbone Open Space, Loveland

Distance: 14.0 miles (round-trip). Difficulty: Moderate. A nice trail on the outskirts of Loveland, this route skirts a series of knobby rock formations that jut out into the sky like vertebrae. The undulating trail includes two 3.5-mile sections that meander through grasslands and a variety of rock outcroppings. (970) 679-4570, www.co.larimer.co.us/parks/bbone.htm.

Spring Creek Trail is one of two paved uninterrupted running paths that runs through the heart of Fort Collins.

5. North Lone Pine Trail, Red Feather Lakes

Distance: 8.8 miles (round-trip). Difficulty: Moderate). The North Lone Pine Trail is an out-and-back backcountry route that begins about 3 miles from the end of Red Feather Lakes Road about an hour northwest of Fort Collins. This heavily forested route climbs gradually as it follows (and occasionally crosses) North Lone Pine Creek. The end of the trail offers pleasing views of the peaks in the Rawah Wilderness. (970) 498-1100, www.fs.fed.us/r2/arnf.

Jon Sinclair: Over 40 and Going Strong

Few U.S. road runners have achieved the success of Fort Collins's Jon Sinclair. In the 1980s and early 1990s, Sinclair was one of the world's best road racers—from 5k to the marathon. In fact, according to *Runner's World* magazine, he has more victories and top-five finishes than any other runner in the world.

Sinclair has been a U.S. champion in cross-country and for the 10,000-meter run on the track and a U.S. record holder for 5k and 12k. His list of major road racing wins includes the Virginia 10 Miler, Atlanta's Peachtree 10k and the Bloomsday 12k in Spokane, Washington. But even more awe-inspiring are his efforts since turning 40 and becoming a masters competitor. Sinclair, who turned 44 in 2002, has twice run sub-1:10 at the Las Vegas Half Marathon, and in 2002 ran 14:52 for 5k at California's Carlsbad 5000.

Sinclair's running career started in the late 1970s, when he was a standout at Colorado State University. He's played a key role in the Fort Collins running community ever since, as a runner, coach and race organizer.

"I came to Fort Collins in 1975, when I was 17 years old, and never left," he says. "I've never found a better place to train."

Sinclair often runs the trails in the foothills west of Fort Collins, including those near Horsetooth Reservoir and Lory State Park, as well as the gravel farm roads east of Fort Collins. He says his favorite place to run in the area is Old Flowers Road about 25 minutes west of Fort Collins.

Sinclair and fellow Fort Collins runner Kent Oglesby are partners in a coaching service called Anaerobic Management. They coach about 50 runners around Colorado and the rest of the U.S., ranging from beginners to Olympic hopefuls.

"I've always enjoyed coaching people," Sinclair says. "It's a way of staying in the sport. And it's been really fun because I have people who are elite runners that keep me in the competitive side of running. But I also have people who are first-time marathoners, so I get to help people who are just starting out, too."

In 2002, Sinclair and Steve Cathcart, co-owner of the Fort Collins Runners Roost store, started the nonprofit Northern Colorado Running Foundation with funds from the inaugural Fort Collins Old Town Marathon. The goal of the nonprofit is to be able to help out other races in the community and start a youth cross-country racing circuit, Sinclair says.

Visit www.anaerobic.net for more info about Anaerobic Management.

Front Range North Running Resources

Track Facilities

Northern Colorado boasts several exceptional all-weather track facilities, including three in Fort Collins. Both Colorado State University (970-491-5434, www.csurams.com) and the University of Northern Colorado (970-351-2534, http://uncbears.ocsn.com) host several track meets each spring. While all of the track facilities listed below are publicly owned, each has its own rules for public usage that should be followed.

*Colorado State University, Jack Christiansen Track, just west of College Ave. between University Ave. and Pitkin St in Fort Collins.
* University of Northern Colorado, Nottingham Field, just north of the intersection of Sixth Ave. and 20th St. in Greeley.
* Fort Collins High School, 3400 Lambkin Way, Fort Collins
* Longmont High School, 1040 Sunset St., Longmont
* Loveland High School, 920 West 29th St., Loveland
* Poudre High School, 201 Impala Dr., Fort Collins
* Skyline High School, 600 East Mountain View Ave., Longmont
* Thompson Valley High School, 1669 Eagle Dr., Loveland

Group Runs/Running Clubs

Bells Running Club

meets on Wednesday evenings at Bells Running shop (3620 West 10th St., Greeley) for 4- to 7-mile runs and also organizes speed workouts through the year at Westmore Park. Call (970) 356-6964 for details.

Fort Collins Hash House Harriers

is a group that meets once a month for adventure runs (also known as "hashes"). Call (970) 484-9377 for details.

Fort Collins Running Club

has been active since 1971, making it one of Colorado's oldest running clubs. It organizes group runs (3 to 4 miles) on Thursday nights (5:30 P.M. in winter, 6:30 P.M. in summer) from the Foot of the Rockies (West), 1205 W. Elizabeth St., Fort Collins. It also organizes long runs on Sunday mornings from Gate 4 of CSU's Hughes Stadium and hosts the Tortoise & Hare Race Series the first Sunday of every month. Races range from 4k to 13 miles, and slower runners are allowed to begin first. Call (970) 493-4675 or visit www.footoftherockies.com.

Horsetooth Harriers Running Club

meets Sundays mornings at Runners Roost in Fort Collins and Tuesday evenings at the CSU outdoor track for interval workouts. (Note: There was talk in late 2002 about this club merging with the Fort Collins Running Club.) Call (970) 224-9114.

Longmont Running Club

meets at 8:30 A.M. at Golden Ponds Park, near Hover Road and Third Street. Call (303) 776-1526.

Loveland Road Runners

is a club that meets for group runs on Saturdays and Sundays at various locations in Loveland and gathers for track workouts at Loveland High School on Tuesday evenings in the spring, summer and fall. Visit www.lovelandroadrunners.com.

Northern Colorado Triathlon Club

meets for open swims, group runs and rides throughout the year. Call (970) 416-8530 or visit http://go.to/triathlon.

Running/Fitness Retailers

Bells Running

3620 West 10th St., Greeley
(970) 356-6964

Bike-N-Hike

1136 Main St., Longmont
(303) 772-5105

Eastern Mountain Sports

101 East Foothills Pkwy., Fort Collins
(970) 223-6511
www.ems.com

Foot of the Rockies (West)

1205 W. Elizabeth St., Suite A, Fort Collins
(970) 493-4675
www.footoftherockies.com

Foot of the Rockies (East)

150 E. Harmony Rd., Unit 2C, Fort Collins

(970) 377-8005

www.footoftherockies.com

Loveland Cycle & Fitness

524 N. Cleveland Ave., Loveland

(970) 667-1943

REI

4025 S. College Ave., Fort Collins

(970) 223-0123

www.rei.com

Runners Roost

902 W. Drake Rd., Fort Collins

(970) 493-6701

www.runnersroost.com

Sneakers

257 East 29th St., Loveland

(970) 663-4880

Photo by Phil Mislinski/www.pmimage.com

Matt Carpenter descends Barr Trail enroute to another win in the Pikes Peak Marathon.

Front Range South

Colorado Springs, Franktown, Manitou Springs, Monument, Pueblo, Woodland Park

Majestic Pikes Peak has drawn visitors from around the world for more than a century and a half. The giant mountain that looms over Colorado Springs and Manitou Springs is the 31st tallest peak in Colorado, and one of the only summits in the world that can be reached by train, car, bicycle and foot. More important, the presence of Pikes Peak makes the Colorado Springs area the only large urban market in the U.S. with a major mountain within minutes of downtown. The fact that the annual Pikes Peak Marathon is the fourth oldest marathon in the country is a testament to the generations of hearty people who have lived here.

Many locals have run Barr Trail to the summit dozens of times; others have never made it past Barr Camp. But the Peak, as locals call it, is ever-present in the local running community, continually serving as an inspiration to runners of all abilities. Arguably America's most famous mountain, it plays a role in local weather, serves as the site of several trail races and stands as a symbol of the challenge, adventure and freedom that runners universally cherish.

The southern Front Range has some of the best races in Colorado—especially the Pikes Peak Ascent and Marathon and Barr Trail Mountain Race—as well as some of the most dedicated running clubs anywhere. From Franktown to Pueblo, there are dozens of great places to run in this region, but virtually every trail, path and park pay homage to the Peak—either by running in its shadows or by offering breathtaking views.

Barr Trail Run 42

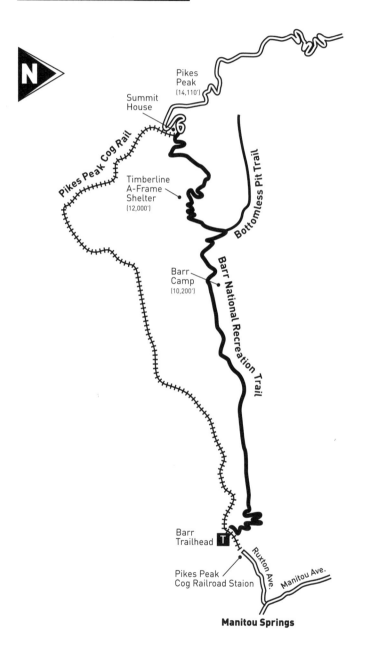

N

Pikes
Peak
(14,110')

Summit
House

Pikes Peak Cog Rail

Bottomless Pit Trail

Timberline
A-Frame
Shelter
(12,000')

Barr
Camp
(10,200')

Barr National Recreation Trail

Barr
Trailhead T

Ruxton Ave.

Manitou Ave.

Pikes Peak
Cog Railroad Staion

Manitou Springs

Barr Trail (Manitou Springs)
Run 42

Distance/Terrain: 11.25 miles on singletrack dirt and gravel trails and a bit of gravel fire road.

Difficulty: Moderate to hard. The higher you go, the harder it gets!

Elevation Change: Extreme.

Trailhead: The trailhead is located off Ruxton Avenue west of the town of Manitou Springs, just beyond the Pikes Peak Cog Railway Depot. The parking lot is usually crowded on weekends, so if you can't find a spot, you'll have to find parking down the road in Manitou Springs. (Do not park in the railway parking lots, even if you're intending to ride the train down. The parking lots are dedicated for round-trip ticket holders only.) Restrooms are available at the trailhead, Barr Camp and the summit.

Dogs: Yes, but they must be on a leash.

Running Strollers: Don't even think about it.

Route Description: The most extraordinary running trail anywhere in America, it's a must-do for experienced trail runners. Rising nearly 7,500 feet in 11.25 miles from the 6,770-foot elevation of the trailhead to the 14,110-foot summit of Pikes Peak, it is a trail without equal. Barr passes through three ecological life zones (montane, spruce-fir and alpine) and is home to a wide variety of wildlife, and weather can change dramatically from the bottom to top. Given the length of the trail and dramatic change in climate and altitude, running the entire trail to the top is not something to be taking lightly.

The trail varies in steepness on its way to the summit, ranging from mildly rolling terrain between 8,500 and 10,000 feet to lung-busting steeps in the final 3.0 miles to the summit. The trail is surprisingly smooth most of the way, but there are places too steep to run for even the fittest of runners (with a few exceptions). Don't knock yourself out. Whether you're out there for fun or entered in one of the races, remember that it's a big mountain and you're never going to conquer it. Run within yourself, and stop to enjoy the views every now and then, and you'll eventually get to the top (or to Barr Camp at 10,200 feet, if that's your destination) and wind up with a satisfying experience.

Because of the change in elevation and potential severity of the conditions that can be encountered, no one should attempt running on Barr Trail without serious preparation, altitude training and knowledge of the mountain. Extra water, clothing and snack food are a must, as the 22.5-mile round-trip can take five to eight hours to complete. Keep in mind the temperature can easily be 40 degrees cooler on top of the mountain than at the trailhead. As the trail climbs, there are few places to take shelter aside from Barr Camp and an A-frame shelter near tree line (about 12,000 feet). Barr Trail also intersects several other trails, but all intersections are well-marked and shouldn't lead to any confusion.

No one knows more about the Barr Trail and Pikes Peak (especially from a runner's perspective) than mountain running phenom Matt Carpenter of Manitou Springs (see the sidebar on page 199). His extraordinary website (www.skyrunner.com) is chock-full of information about running the trail, the 13.32-mile Pikes Peak Ascent, 26.2-mile Marathon and the 12-mile Barr Trail Mountain Race. The Incline Club (see the "Group Runs" section on page 202) regularly runs on Barr Trail and encourages new members of all abilities. Also, visit the Friends of the Peak website (www.fotp.com) for more information about Pikes Peak.

Alternate Routes: For a unique twist (or if your knees loathe long downhills), consider running the trail up and taking the Pikes Peak Cog Railway back down. It's wise to buy a train ticket at the bottom of the mountain (in other words, before you start). For details, call (719) 685-5401 or visit www.cograilway.com. Instead of going to the top of the mountain, you can connect Manitou Reservoir and French Creek trails on the north side of Barr Trail to create a spectacular 18-mile loop through the Hurricane Natural Area.

Wildlife: Just about everything you can imagine, including deer, elk, bighorn sheep, mountain goats, mountain lions, bears, marmots, ptarmigans and much more.
Weather: The upper reaches of Barr Trail (anywhere from 10,000 to 14,000 feet) are generally not runnable during winter because of heavy snow pack. Conditions at the summit are almost always vastly different (wind, rain, snow, temperatures) than those at the lower sections. Be prepared!
Other Users: Hikers.
Maps: USGS 1:24,000 Map, Pikes Peak Colorado, 1993; U.S. Forest Service Map, Pikes Peak Ranger District; Colorado Springs Pikes Peak 75k Trail & Recreation Map, Second Edition (2002, Sky Terrain).
Contact Info: (719) 636-1602, www.fs.fed.us/r2/psicc/pp/barr.shtml.

Castlewood Canyon (Franktown)
Run 43

Distance/Terrain: About 6.5 miles (round-trip), almost entirely on singletrack dirt
and gravel trails.

Difficulty: Moderate. There are a few short but steep climbs in the park.

Elevation Change: Moderate.

Trailheads: There several parking areas and trail access points from the park's
east entrance (also considered the main entrance), located about 4 miles south
of Franktown on Colorado Highway 83. The west entrance is located about 2.5
miles southwest of Franktown on Castlewood Canyon Road. To reach the park
from I-25, get off at the main Castle Rock exit and take Highway 86 East about
6 miles. Head south on Castlewood Canyon Road to reach the west entrance.
There is a $5 park fee per vehicle. Restrooms are available near both the east
and west entrances.

Dogs: Yes, but you must keep them on a leash at all times.

Running Strollers: No, not advised.

Route Description: Castlewood Canyon State Park, perhaps the best-kept secret
on the Front Range, is a trail-running sanctuary. There is a lot packed into the 6.5-
mile loop around the perimeter of the long and narrow park property, including
soft singletrack trails, panoramic views of the entire Front Range, spectacular
cliffs, waterfalls on bubbling Cherry Creek and the ruins of a stone dam built in
1890. (The dam has been defunct since it burst in 1933 and caused one of the
worst floods in Denver history.)

Starting from the Westside trailhead south of the west entrance, take Cherry
Creek Trail north for a mile as it zigzags toward an old homestead site. Make a
right and descend the aptly named Homestead Trail to the creek, cross the wobbly
wooden bridge and head up the moderately steep Rimrock Trail. Once on top of
the bluffs, the trail is generally flat for about 1.5 miles, which gives you plenty of
time to catch your breath and check out the views. (Just don't get too close to the
edge, because the creek is about 250 feet below.)

The route dips back down on the short, steep and technical Dam Trail, where
it runs into a junction (mile 3.25) with Creek Bottom Trail and Inner Canyon Trail.
Go left and follow Inner Canyon Trail as it climbs slightly along the banks of the
creek. After crossing a wooden bridge, stay on the same trail as it climbs the
southern bluff of the creek on a series of switchbacks and wooden-rail stairs.
After a 0.25-mile of concrete trail, you'll arrive at the Canyon Point trailhead and

Castlewood Canyon Run 43

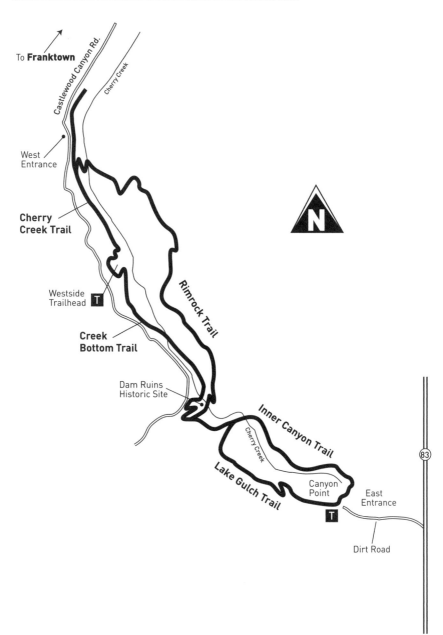

When Castlewood Canyon Dam burst in 1933, Cherry Creek overflowed its banks and eventually flooded downtown Denver.

spectacular views of Pikes Peak (mile 4.5). Take Lake Gulch Trail west from the trailhead's parking lot and follow it as it steadily drops back to the creek. Cross the wooden bridge, take a left, and run back along Inner Canyon Trail, but this time when you get to the three-way junction (mile 5.5), head left (west) toward the creek. Follow Creek Bottom Trail along the banks of the creek, past the crumbling historic dam site and back to the Westside trailhead.

Wildlife: Deer, antelope, skunks, rattlesnakes, foxes, black squirrels and a variety of birds and raptors.

Weather: The park is open year-round and the trails are generally very runnable, except after a big snow. Some trails can be muddy in winter and spring or hold snow and ice several days after a storm.

Other Users: Mountain bikers (only on specified trails), equestrians and hikers.

Map: Castlewood Canyon Map, Colorado State Parks.

Contact Info: (303) 688-5242, www.parks.state.co.us/castlewood/trails.asp.

Columbine Trail Run 44

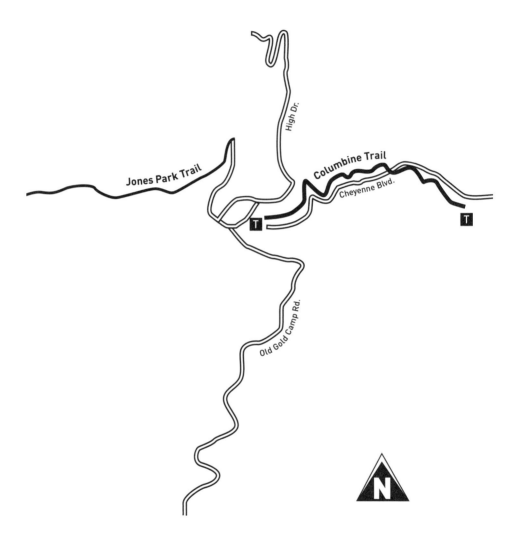

Columbine Trail (Colorado Springs)
Run 44

Distance/Terrain: About 8.0 miles (round-trip) on singletrack dirt and gravel trails.

Difficulty: Moderate. The trail climbs continually to the turnaround point.

Elevation Change: Moderate. The trail rises about 1,100 feet in 4.0 miles.

Trailheads: The main trailhead is located behind the Starsmore Discovery Center at the mouth of North Cheyenne Cañon Park on the west end of Cheyenne Boulevard. The park is open from 5 A.M. to 11 P.M. in summer and from 5 A.M. to 9 P.M. in winter. There are restrooms at the trailhead.

Dogs: Yes, but keep 'em on a leash.

Running Strollers: No.

Route Description: North Cheyenne Cañon Park was once a popular camping ground for Ute Native Americans. Now it's a 1,626-acre park interspersed with trails that make for good uphill-downhill runs. Columbine Trail starts at the mouth of North Cheyenne Cañon and rises about 1,100 feet in 4.0 miles as it climbs to Helen Hunt Falls. Starting from the main trailhead, the trail starts out almost flat for 1.0 mile, shrouded in pine trees along the banks of Cheyenne Creek. But from the second mile on, this run gets more arduous and the footing gets dicier with loose gravel. But as you begin to climb, expansive views unfurl in all directions. The trail levels off a bit during the third mile when it separates from the creek and the road on a series of switchbacks. The trail reconnects with the road and the creek near the Upper Columbine trailhead near Helen Hunt Falls (across the road). After taking a peek at the falls, you've earned the right to zip back down the trail to complete a rewarding 8.0-mile run.

Alternate Routes: Dozens of other trails can be reached from North Cheyenne Cañon, including the trails in nearby Stratton Open Space, Gold Camp Road Trail (see "Other Front Range South Trails" on page 197), Mt. Cutler Trail, Daniels Pass Trail and Jones Park Trail, among others.

Wildlife: Deer, foxes, squirrels, bighorn sheep, snakes and a variety of birds.

Weather: Columbine Trail is well protected from wind, but many of the shady sections below can be muddy or snow-covered during winter and spring.

Other Users: Hikers and mountain bikers.

Maps: North Cheyenne Cañon Map, City of Colorado Springs Parks, Recreation & Cultural Services Department; Colorado Springs Pikes Peak 75k Trail & Recreation Map, Second Edition (2002, Sky Terrain).

Contact Info: (719) 385-6540, www.springsgov.com.

Garden of the Gods   Run 45

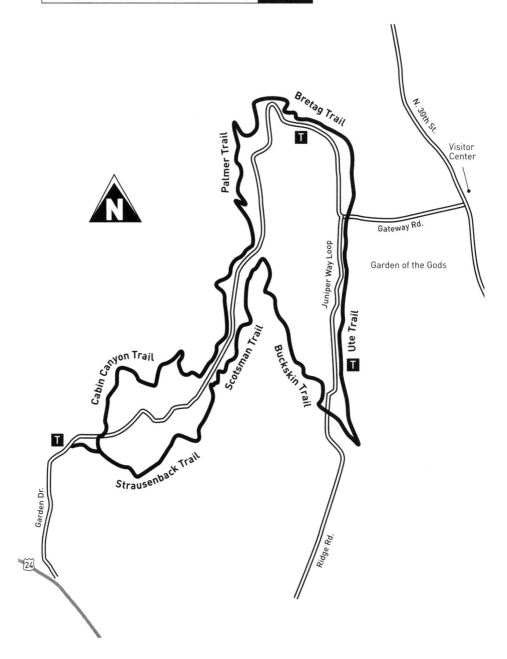

Garden of the Gods (Colorado Springs)
Run 45

Distance/Terrain: 9.0 miles (round-trip) on singletrack dirt trails, concrete walking paths and paved roads.

Difficulty: Easy to moderate. There are unlimited combinations of routes with mild
rolling hills and a few steeps.

Elevation Change: Minimal.

Trailheads: The main park entrance and visitor center is at 1805 N. 30th Street on
the western edge of Colorado Springs. But to avoid some of the tourist traffic, you
might consider parking at the Balanced Rock parking area on Garden Drive at the
southwest corner of the park. Garden of the Gods is open from 5 A.M. to 11 P.M. in
summer and from 5 A.M. to 9 P.M. in winter. Restrooms are available in the park.

Dogs: Dogs are allowed on a six-foot leash; there is one small area south of
Gateway Road and west of 30th Street where dogs can run unleashed.

Running Strollers: Strollers will work on the roads and paved trails but generally
not on the dirt trails.

Route Description: With its striking red rock formations, Garden of the Gods is
unlike anywhere else in Colorado. The 1,392-acre park is a great place to run, if
only for sheer inspiration from the surroundings. Most runs within the park will
take you on a combination of natural trails, concrete paths and paved roads.
Settlers have been enchanted with the area since the 1850s, but ancient pottery
found in the park dates back to A.D. 575 to 900.

Starting from the Balanced Rock parking lot, follow Balanced Rock Trail to
the east, to Cabin Canyon Trail and loop around to Siamese Twins Trail around the
back side of stunning Siamese Twins Rock (mile 1.5). Pick up Palmer Trail and run
it to the north end of the park around the massive North Gateway Rock and past
the main parking area. About 3.5 miles from the parking lot, the Palmer Trail, will
turn into Susan Bretag Trail. Take that route south, crossing the paved park road
(Gateway Road) and continuing on Ute Trail. Here you can take one of a few rolling
mountain bike-accessible trails to your left (east) or right (west) and run Buckskin
Trail through the Scotsman picnic area. Complete your loop by running
Strausenback Loop Trail to the southwest, passing by the Spring Canyon picnic
area and picking up Balance Rock Trail.

The annual Garden of the Gods 10-Mile Run, part of the Pikes Peak Triple
Crown of Running, is held in the park in early June. For more information, visit
www.pikespeakmarathon.org.

Wildlife: Deer, falcons, foxes, bats and a variety of birds and raptors.

Weather: Garden of the Gods is open year-round, and its trails are generally runnable every day of the year. A few of the upper sections can be windy, and some trails can be muddy or snow-packed in winter and spring.

Other Users: Mountain bikers (only on specified trails), equestrians and hikers.

Maps: Garden of the Gods Map, Recreation & Cultural Services Department; Colorado Springs Pikes Peak 75k Trail & Recreation Map, Second Edition (2002, Sky Terrain).

Contact Info: (719) 634-6666, www.gardenofthegods.com.

Monument Trail/Mt. Herman Trail
(Monument)
Run 46

Distance/Terrain: 11.0 miles (round-trip) on singletrack dirt and gravel trails.

Difficulty: Moderate to hard. The final ascent is steep and challenging for runners of all abilities.

Elevation Change: Moderate to extreme. The lower portion of the trail climbs gradually from 7,200 feet, but it can be a grind running the final 3.0 miles out of the North Beaver Creek drainage (about 1,000 feet of climbing).

Trailheads: Drive south past the Mt. Herman trailhead on Nursery Road, go right on Schilling Avenue and near the Forest Service gate at Lindbergh Road.

Dogs: Yes, dogs are allowed, if they're on a leash.

Running Strollers: Nope.

Route Description: At 9,063 feet, Mt. Herman is one of the taller summits on the horizon immediately north of Pikes Peak. Reaching the top can be a challenge, but stunning views of the plains and fun downhill running make the trudge rewarding. Starting from the gate, the trail begins on a gravel road but turns to the left (at the trailhead sign-in) after about 0.25 mile. Take the singletrack route to the south, veering right at the first unmarked fork in the trail that you'll come across after 150 yards. Follow the sand and gravel trail as it climbs gradually through scrub oak to another fork in the road (mile 1.5). This time, veer left and continue climbing up the side of a knoll, where the trail turns to the south and is strewn with rocks and roots.

Monument Trail/Mt. Herman Trail Run 46

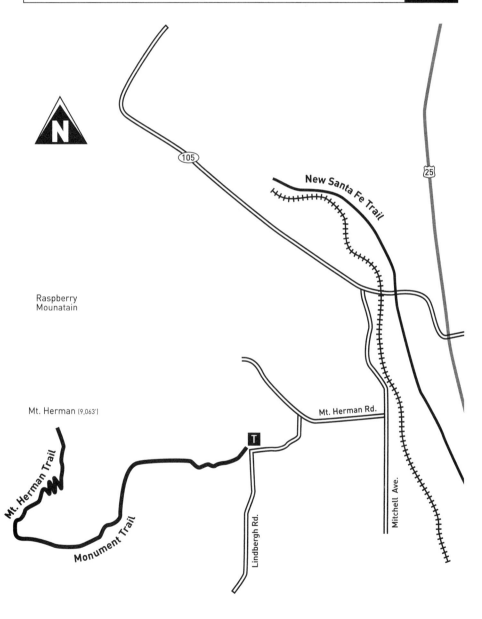

After crossing the pine-covered knoll, the trail begins to roll up and down as it heads into the North Beaver Creek drainage. Following a ridge below (and eventually next to) Mt. Herman Road, the trail follows the creek upstream and then crosses the road (mile 3.5) near the Mt. Herman trailhead. The final 2.0 miles to the top of the mountain include several switchbacks before flattening out and following a ridge to the highpoint on the summit.

Once you reach the top, retrace your steps for your return, which is mostly downhill, except for a mild incline over that pine-covered knoll. As your prize for reaching the top, stop by Colorado General Mercantile (just east of the railroad tracks in the town of Monument) for a homemade sandwich or a double-decker ice cream cone.

Wildlife: Deer, elk, mountain lions, squirrels, raccoons and many birds.
Weather: The top of Mt. Herman and the higher portions of Monument Trail can be icy and snowy in winter. In spring, there's plenty of sticky mud on the trail.
Other Users: Horseback riders, mountain bikers and hikers.
Map: USGS 1:24,000 Map, Pikes Peak Colorado, 1986; Pikes Peak Ranger District Map, U.S. Forest Service.
Contact Info: (719) 636-1602, www.fs.fed.us/r2/psicc/pp.

Palmer Park (Colorado Springs)
Run 47

Distance/Terrain: Up to 25.0 miles or more (one way) on a variety of narrow and wide trails.
Difficulty: Easy to hard. The park offers something for everyone.
Elevation Change: Minimal to moderate. You can climb as little or as much as your heart and lungs desire.
Trailheads: There are several places to start a run, including the east entrance on Paseo Road at Chelton Road; the southeast entrance on Maizeland Road just west of Academy Boulevard; and at various picnic areas, overlooks and trailheads in the park. Restrooms are located throughout Palmer Park, which is open from 5 A.M. to 11 P.M. in summer and from 5 A.M. to 9 P.M. in winter.
Dogs: Yes, but your pup must be on a leash at all times.
Running Strollers: Generally not recommended.

Palmer Park Run 47

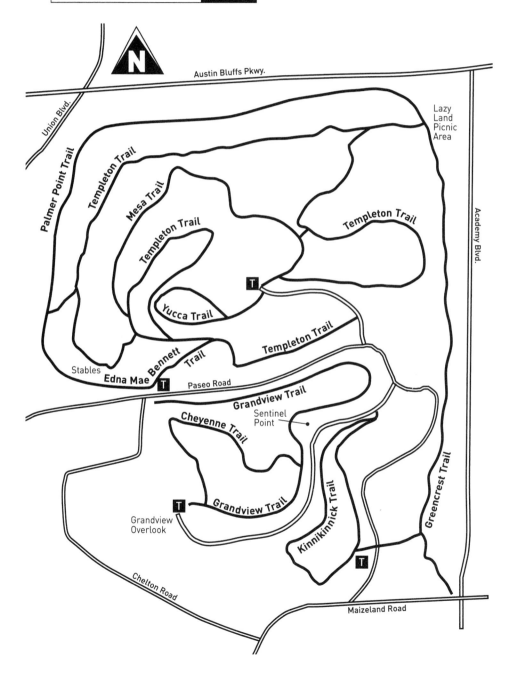

Palmer Park in Colorado Springs has some of the most diverse terrain of any park along the Front Range.

Route Description: Palmer Park is arguably the best urban park along the Front Range, especially among areas not adjacent to the foothills. It is named after General William Jackson Palmer, who founded Colorado Springs in 1871 when he brought the Denver & Rio Grande Western Railway south from Denver. The 737-acre park, one of the original seven parks Palmer donated to the city, is an epic running and mountain bike playground, with more than 25 miles of trails (and a few more miles of rogue "social" trails created by short-cutting).

The park consists of several pine-covered rocky crags interspersed by several high mesas. With a series of easy, intermediate and advanced trails, Palmer Park is ideal for everything from short runs to ultra-distance workouts where you loop back to your car for water or snacks. The park allows for an easy escape from the hustle and bustle of Colorado Springs and offers great views of the city and the mountains that border it to the west, especially Pikes Peak.

There are two minor drawbacks to running at Palmer Park: There are almost too many trails (believe it or not), and the maps posted at the trailheads don't help much. If you're going to run at Palmer Park, either go with a local familiar with the park or pick up a copy of the Palmer Park Trail System Map ($10, Sanborn Map Company) at a local running shop or outdoor store. Made from aerial photography, it is extremely useful for planning runs and finding your car. (There is a city map available online at www.springsgov.com, but it's just as convoluted as the maps posted at the trailheads.) The Yucca Flats trailhead in the center of the park is where a lot of runners meet, if only because it affords a lot of options for fun loop runs.

Wildlife: Deer, squirrels, raccoons, garter snakes and a variety of birds.

Weather: The trails are accessible year-round. Some of the upper trails can be susceptible to winds and a few can be muddy or snow- and ice-packed for brief stretches during winter and spring.

Other Users: Mountain bikers, horseback riders, hikers and picnickers.

Map: Palmer Park Map, City of Colorado Springs Parks, Recreation & Cultural Services Department.

Contact Info: (719) 385-5940, www.springsgov.com.

Pikes Peak Greenway and Fountain Creek Trail
(Colorado Springs)
Run 48

Distance/Terrain: Up to 30.0 miles (round-trip) on wide dirt trails and concrete bike paths through the heart of Colorado Springs.

Difficulty: Easy.

Elevation Change: Minimal.

Trailheads: There are numerous places to pick up the trail, including Monument Valley Park in the heart of the city, the Edmondson trailhead on Woodmen Road, Goose Gossage Park, Dorchester Park and the El Pomar Youth Sports Park. Restrooms are available at some of the trailheads and at parks along the trail.

Dogs: Yes, dogs are allowed, but they must be leashed at all times.

Running Strollers: Yes, it's a great place to run with the young ones in a stroller!

Route Description: The most popular route in Colorado Springs—especially when it comes to running—the Pikes Peak Greenway and Fountain Creek Trail combination offers an ideal escape from traffic while adding a touch of greenery and history. While the region has epic mountain routes like Barr Trail and Waldo Canyon, the Pikes Peak Greenway and Fountain Creek Trail form a route that really ties the

Pikes Peak Greenway and Fountain Creek Trail

Run 48

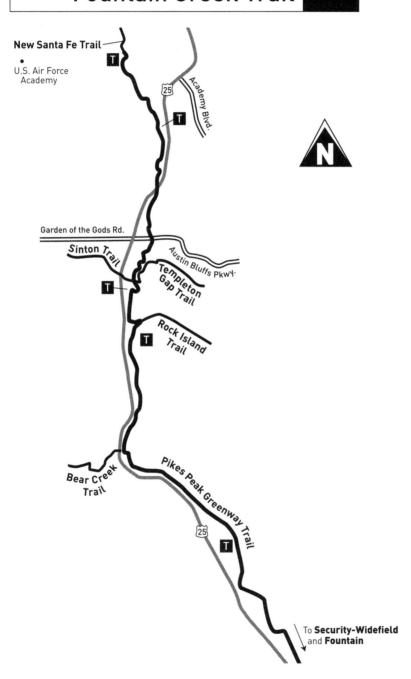

New Santa Fe Trail

U.S. Air Force Academy

Academy Blvd.

Garden of the Gods Rd.

Sinton Trail

Austin Bluffs Pkwy.

Templeton Gap Trail

Rock Island Trail

Bear Creek Trail

Pikes Peak Greenway Trail

To **Security-Widefield** and **Fountain**

local trail system together and makes the area one of the top urban trail centers in the U.S. The two trails provide many glimpses of Colorado Springs, as it passes industrial and residential areas, historical railroad lines, the campus of Colorado College and more.

The trails are virtually flat the entire way through town, making them perfect for long leisurely runs, fartlek workouts and time trials. They meander on both sides of the creek and feature mileage markers to give you a relatively accurate length of your run.

Once a month throughout the year, the Pikes Peak Road Runners hold the unique and popular Nielson Challenge—1-mile and 2-mile time-handicapped races—in North Monument Valley Park, along the greenway. The first half of the 12k Summer Roundup Trail Run (early July), part of the Triple Crown of Running, is run on Pikes Peak Greenway. Visit www.pikespeakmarathon.org for more details.

Alternate Routes: The Pikes Peak Greenway and Fountain Creek Trail connect with about a dozen other routes in Colorado Springs. An unlimited number of long runs (with numerous support points) can be organized from these two trails. By combining the pair with Santa Fe Trail to the north (see the write-up in the "Other Front Range South Trails" section on page 197), you could conceivably run more than 30 miles in one direction with very few road crossings. (There are a few drinking fountains located along the route, as well as several nearby convenience stores where you can refill your supply of water and energy snacks.)

Wildlife: Deer, raccoons, foxes, squirrels, frogs and a variety of birds.
Weather: The greenway and trail are fairly well protected from wind and, because they are flat and wide, are rarely obstructed by mud, snow or ice.
Other Users: Cyclists, walkers, hikers and equestrians.
Maps: Pikes Peak Greenway Trail Map, City of Colorado Springs Parks, Recreation & Cultural Services; Colorado Springs Pikes Peak 75k Trail & Recreation Map, Second Edition (2002, Sky Terrain).
Contact Info: (719) 385-5940; www.springsgov.com, http://adm.elpasoco.com/Parks/prktrail.asp.

The flat and fast Pikes Peak Greenway is a great place for tempo runs and fartlek workouts.

Rampart Reservoir Trail
(Woodland Park)
Run 49

Distance/Terrain: 14.0 miles (round-trip) on singletrack dirt and gravel trails and wide fire roads.

Difficulty: Moderate. It has flat sections mixed in with plenty of rollers, dips and gullies.

Elevation Change: Minimal.

Trailheads: Rampart Reservoir Recreation Area is located about 18 miles northwest of Colorado Springs on Rampart Range Road. You can reach the reservoir by taking Rampart Range Road west from the back side of Garden of the Gods. Otherwise you can drive to Woodland Park, take Baldwin Road to Loy Creek Road, and pick up Rampart Range Road. From there, the reservoir is about 3 miles to the south. The best place to start the run is from the Rainbow Gulch trailhead along Rampart Range Road. If you drive into the recreation area, you'll have to pay a $4 fee. There are restrooms at several places inside the recreation area but not at the trailhead.

Dogs: Dogs must be on a leash at all times.

Running Strollers: No.

Route Description: The trail around Rampart Reservoir makes for a scenic, mostly shaded and very satisfying trail run. The terrain is mildly technical and hilly, but it's an ideal place for runners of all abilities. The trail is situated at about 9,000 feet above sea level, so you might find yourself slightly more taxed than usual for a long run. The 50-acre reservoir, which holds 13 billion gallons of water, supplies water to homes and businesses in Colorado Springs.

Starting from the Rainbow Gulch trailhead, enter the gate and begin the 1.5-mile descent on the fire road on the north side of the spillway. At the bottom of the gulch, continue straight ahead at the fork in the trail (avoiding the bridge on the right) and begin the 11.0-mile singletrack loop around the reservoir in a clockwise direction. When you first glance the reservoir, it doesn't appear that the loop could be that long, but the trail follows several fingers along the shore, thus extending its distance.

The trail around the north side of the reservoir rolls gently as it weaves in and out of conifer forests, aspen groves and a few open meadows. After passing the intersection with Backdoor Trail (mile 7), you'll eventually reach the 3,400-foot-long dam (mile 8.25), where you'll need to hop on the road (and get a stunning

Rampart Reservoir Trail   Run 49

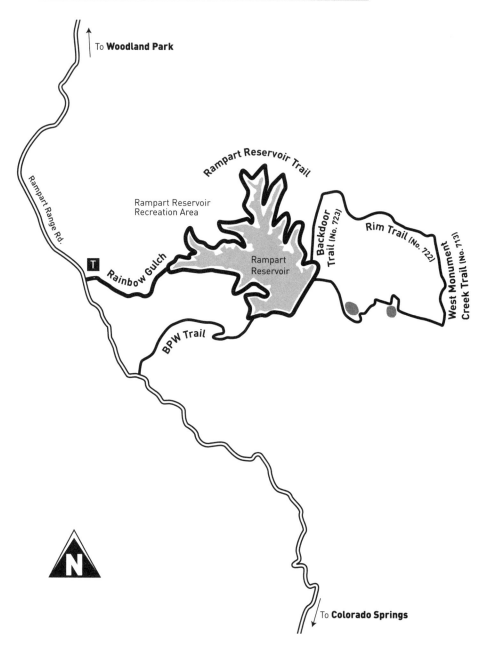

To **Woodland Park**

Rampart Range Rd.

Rampart Reservoir Trail

Rampart Reservoir
Recreation Area

Rainbow Gulch

T

Rampart
Reservoir

Backdoor Trail (No. 723)

Rim Trail (No. 722)

West Monument Creek Trail (No. 713)

BPW Trail

N

To **Colorado Springs**

view of the north slope of Pikes Peak) and run the length of the curving dam road to the Wildcat Wayside sign on the other side. Pick up the trail to the right (behind the sign) and continue the loop on the south side of the reservoir. The trail runs into some technical terrain and an area known as The Notch, a narrow passage through a series of large rocks (mile 10.0). From there, the trail cruises around one last finger and then it's smooth sailing along the southern shore back to the bridge (mile 12.5) and the junction with Rainbow Gulch. The final 1.5-mile trudge up Rainbow Gulch draw can be tiresome, but it's the perfect way to end a very satisfying run.

Alternate Routes: There are several other trails you can reach from Rampart Reservoir. To add an extra 5.0 miles to the above loop, take the Backdoor Trail (No. 723), which starts at the north side of the reservoir to Stanley Rim Trail (No. 722). Follow that to West Monument Creek Trail (No. 713), but be sure to take a right toward Northfield Reservoir or you'll wind up in Colorado Springs. Circle around Northfield and Nichols reservoirs, and you'll end up at the Rampart Reservoir dam.

Wildlife: Deer, foxes, elk, skunks, squirrels, raccoons, raptors, birds and a variety of trout (in the reservoir).

Weather: The trail, which runs close to the water line in many places, can be muddy and soggy at times, even submerged. Although accessible year-round, the trail is often covered in snow in winter. While an ideal cross-country ski and snowshoe trail, it can be hard to run in running shoes in winter.

Other Users: Mountain bikers, hikers, fishermen and picnickers.

Maps: Rampart Reservoir Recreation Area Map, U.S. Forest Service Pikes Peak Ranger District; Colorado Springs Pikes Peak 75k Trail & Recreation Map, Second Edition (2002, Sky Terrain).

Contact Info: (719) 636-1602, www.fs.fed.us/r2/psicc/pp/ramparttrail.shtml.

Section 16 and Palmer Trail Loop

Run 50

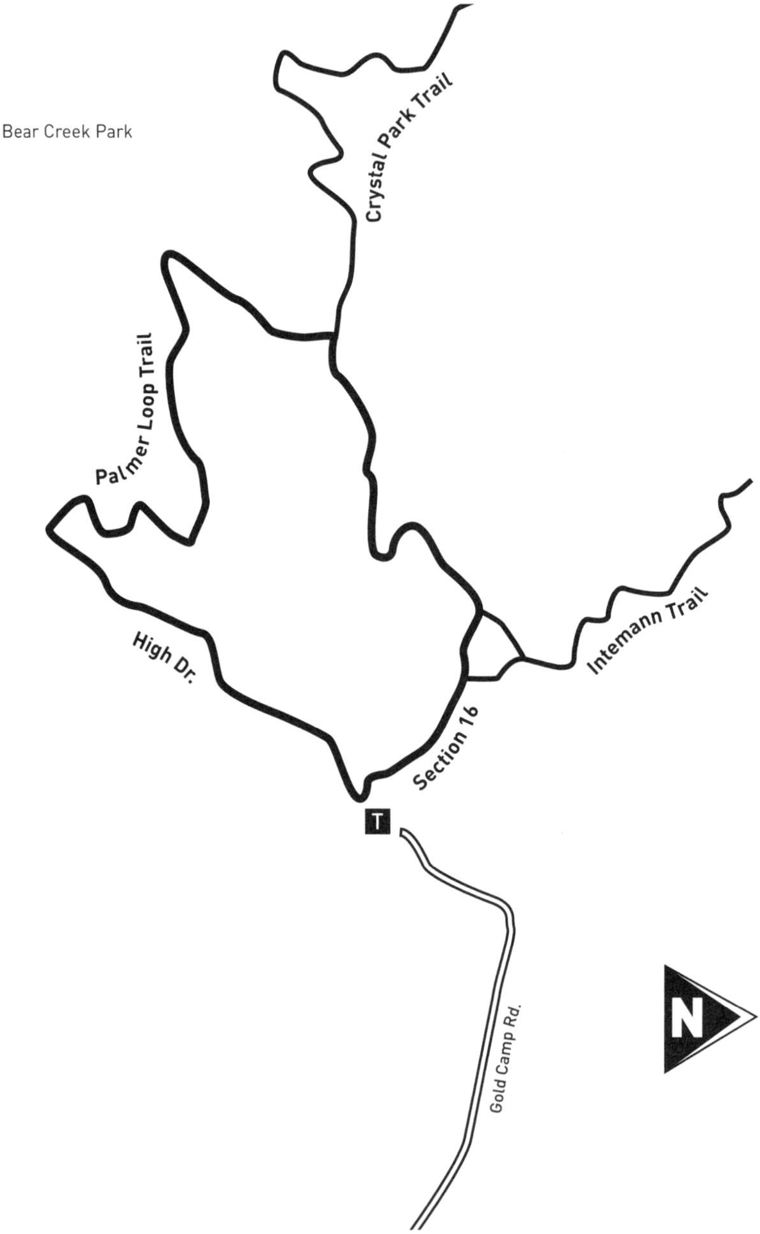

Bear Creek Park

Crystal Park Trail

Palmer Loop Trail

Manitou Springs

Intemann Trail

High Dr.

Section 16

T

Gold Camp Rd.

N

Section 16 and Palmer Trail Loop
(Colorado Springs)
Run 50

Distance/Terrain: 5.75 miles (round-trip) primarily on singletrack dirt and gravel trails and fire roads.

Difficulty: Moderate to hard.

Elevation Change: Moderate. The trail gains about 1,600 feet in 2 to 3 miles (depending on which direction you run) from the trailhead to the high point of the loop.

Trailheads: The Section 16 trailhead is located near the intersection of Gold Camp Road and High Drive west of Bear Creek Park. Take Lower Gold Camp Road west from Bear Creek, go straight through the four-way stop, and you'll find the trailhead about 1.0 mile ahead on the right.

Dogs: Yes, dogs are allowed but must be leashed at all times.

Running Strollers: No.

Route Description: Located in the foothills south of Manitou Springs, this loop is relatively short in length but not in grandeur. It is a classic, heavily wooded singletrack trail with great views, a stream crossing, arduous climbs and fun descents.

From the trailhead, begin running southwest along Gold Camp Road and turn right on High Drive (Gold Camp Road peels off to the east after about 0.5 mile). About 1.0 mile from the trailhead, look for a small metal gate along the road on the right. The single-track Palmer Trail runs north in a straight line for 0.25 mile, but then begins a series of switchbacks that take you on a gradual climb to about the 2.0-mile mark of your run.

The trail angles into the Hunters Run Creek drainage, eventually crossing the creek and angling back out along the north side of the drainage. You'll continue climbing for another 0.5 mile or so, but just after you begin a descent from the high point of the run, you'll come to a fork with Section 16 trail (mile 3.3). Take the right fork, which will send you on a devilish downhill on the loose gravel of Section 16 trail. Near the bottom of the descent, you'll zip through a small clearing (mile 4.5) and then bypass a cut-off trail that connects with the Paul Intemann Memorial Nature Trail. Continue on the main trail and you'll wind up back at the trailhead.

Alternate Routes: Several other routes can be reached from the Section 16 trail-head, including a peaceful 5.0-mile out-and-back run on the Paul Intemann Memorial Nature Trail.

Wildlife: Deer, foxes, skunks and bears.

Weather: The route is fairly protected from wind and inclement weather, but it can be muddy in sections during spring and snowy and icy during winter.

Other Users: Mountain bikers and hikers.

Maps: 1:24,000 Map, Manitou Springs, Colorado, 1994; U.S. Forest Service Map, Pikes Peak Ranger District.

Contact Info: (719) 520-6375, http://adm.elpasoco.com/Parks/prktrail.asp, www.trailsandopenspaces.org.

Waldo Canyon Loop
(Manitou Springs)
Run 51

Distance/Terrain: 6.8 miles (round-trip) on soft singletrack dirt and gravel trails.

Difficulty: Moderate.

Elevation Change: Moderate. The trail climbs about 1,600 feet in 3.0 to 3.5 miles of running from the trailhead. The high point of the trail is about 8,400 feet.

Trailheads: The trailhead is located northwest of Manitou Springs off U.S. Highway 24.

Dogs: Dogs are allowed but must be leashed at all times.

Running Strollers: Nope.

Route Description: Waldo Canyon Loop is the most frequented trail in the U.S. Forest Service Pikes Peak Ranger District and also one of the most popular running trails in the Colorado Springs area. It offers panoramic views of Pikes Peak, several stream crossings, open prairie and an array of wildflowers in spring and summer. It's also the former site of the Waldo Hog Farm.

Starting from the trailhead, the route begins with a series of switchbacks and wooden-rail stairs. The climb mellows slightly and then the trail drops down to a creek drainage (mile 2.0), where you'll reach a sign that says "Waldo Loop." Go left and follow the wooded trail along the creek; the trail gets steeper as it ascends to the top of the canyon. The trail crosses the creek five times before turning sharply to the right and then swoops left near the top of the canyon. The trail begins its descent on the back side of the loop through forested terrain and open prairie. Footing on the descent is technical, with many rocks, roots and other obstacles to avoid. After twisting and turning in all directions, the trail eventually connects back

Waldo Canyon Loop `Run 51`

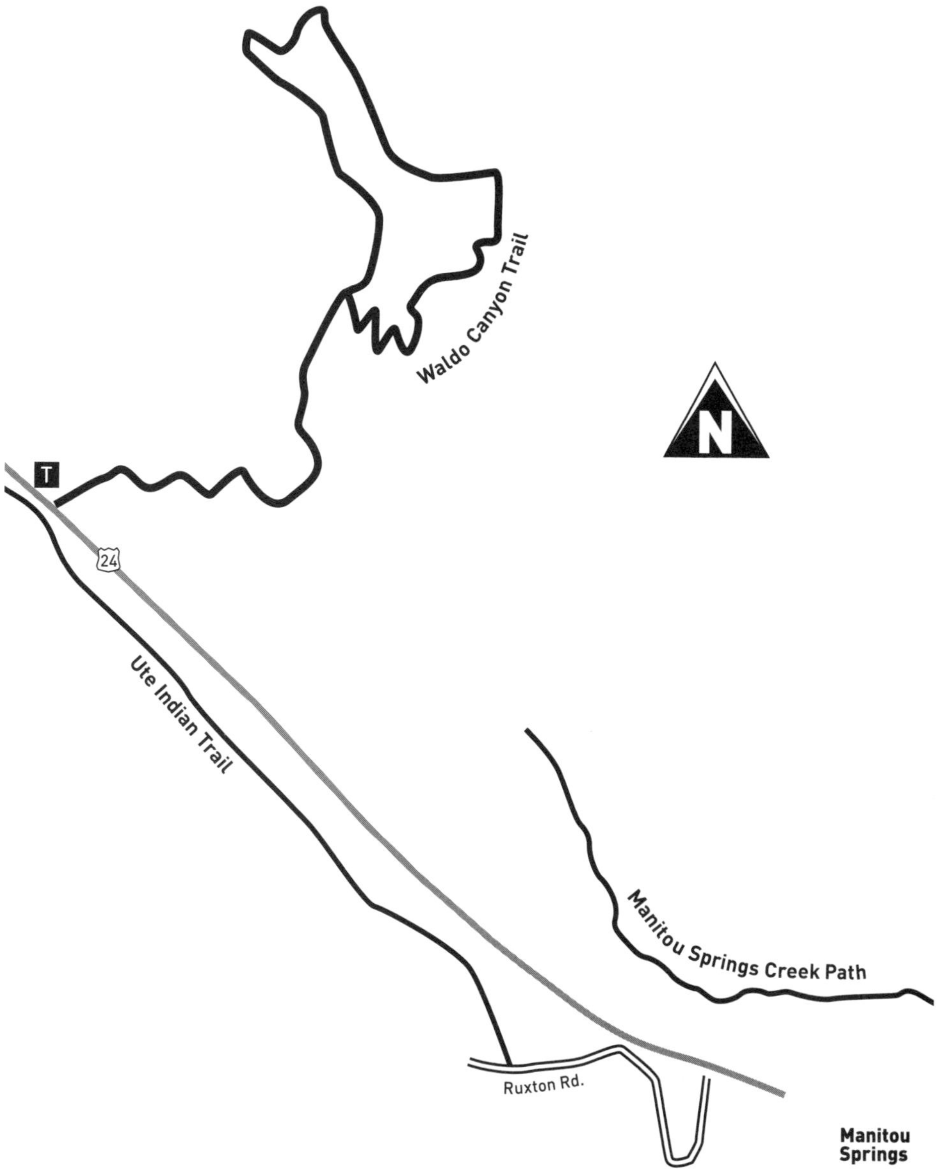

Waldo Canyon Trail

Ute Indian Trail

24

Manitou Springs Creek Path

Ruxton Rd.

Manitou Springs

T

to the fork where you first saw the Waldo Loop sign. Head back down to the trail-head to complete one of the most exhilarating trail runs along the Front Range.

Alternate Routes: For an added challenge and 7.5 more miles of running, start at Soda Springs Park in Manitou Springs and run up the mild ascent of Ute Pass Trail (also known as Ute Indian Trail) northwest to Long Ranch Road. Hang a right, and continue the run from the Waldo Canyon trailhead on the north side of U.S. Highway 24. Complete the loop, and return to the park, and you will have knocked off about 14.5 miles.

Wildlife: Deer, bighorn sheep, foxes, skunks, squirrels, snakes and a variety of birds and raptors.

Weather: The trail is runnable year-round, but there is often ice in the bottom of Waldo Canyon during winter. Running the loop clockwise during winter is advised in order to run up the ice.

Other Users: Hikers, mountain bikers and equestrians.

Maps: U.S. Forest Service Map, Pikes Peak Ranger District; Colorado Springs Pikes Peak 75k Trail & Recreation Map, Second Edition (2002, Sky Terrain).

Contact Info: (719) 636-1602, www.fs.usda.gov/r2/psicc/pp/waldotrail.shtml.

Other Front Range South Trails

1. New Santa Fe Trail, Colorado Springs

Distance: 12.5 miles (one way). Difficulty: Easy. The new Santa Fe Trail is a wide dirt and gravel trail that connects Palmer Lake to the Pikes Peak Greenway and Fountain Creek Trail that run through Colorado Springs. It's an ideal place for long runs of either the out-and-back or point-to-point variety (with a prearranged ride, of course). It offers close-up views of the U.S. Air Force Academy and distant panoramas of Pikes Peak. Dogs are allowed on a leash. (Note: The section adjacent to the Academy closes during heightened Homeland Security alerts.) (719) 520-6375, http://adm.elpasoco.com/Parks/prktrail.asp.

2. Falcon Trail, Colorado Springs

Distance: 12 miles (round-trip). Difficulty: Easy to moderate. This 12-mile loop is an idyllic retreat that follows the perimeter of the U.S. Air Force Academy on the north end of Colorado Springs. But given the security measures following the 9/11 attacks, the Academy was closed to all visitors. Prior to the closure, dogs were permitted on a leash. Call the visitor center at (719) 333-4040 for updated information.

3. Gold Camp Road Trail, Colorado Springs

Distance: Up to 8.0 miles (one way). Difficulty: Easy. Gold Camp Road is a mountain road that follows the route of a former narrow gauge railroad that served gold mines in Cripple Creek. The wide dirt trail climbs at a very slight grade from 7,500 to 9,000 feet as it winds its way across Cheyenne Mountain, making it perfect for long mountain runs with very little vehicular traffic. Dogs are allowed on a leash. (719) 636-1602, www.fs.fed.us/r2/psicc/pp/goldcamp.shtml.

4. Fox Run Regional Park, Colorado Springs

Distance: 3.0 miles (loop). Difficulty: Easy. Located in northeast Colorado Springs, this park offers a short pine-shrouded loop on rolling hills. It's a nice place to get in a short run when you don't feel like dodging traffic on the roads. Dogs are allowed on a leash. (719) 520-6375. http://adm.elpasoco.com/Parks/r_parks/frrp/Frrp.asp.

5. River Trail System, Pueblo

Distance: up to 35 miles (one-way). Difficulty: Easy. A concrete path that runs from Lake Pueblo State Park on the Arkansas River to the University of Southern Colorado near Fountain Creek, it's an ideal place to run fast or slow. For an urban path, it offers a lot to see (especially in the Historic Arkansas Riverwalk) and plenty of options for long runs. Dogs are allowed on a leash. (719) 566-1745, www.pueblo.us.

The old Mt. Manitou Scenic Incline Railway used to run up this steep grade. In the 1990s, Matt Carpenter co-founded The Incline Club, a running group that started by running up this 2,400-foot, near-vertical trail.

Matt Carpenter: King of the Mountain

N o one is more familiar with the well-worn Barr Trail that winds to the 14,110-foot summit of Pikes Peak than Matt Carpenter. The Manitou Springs resident detests the "King of the Mountain" title that so many have placed on him, but it fits. He has made a career running that trail for the past 10 years, winning the Pikes Peak Ascent and Pikes Peak Marathon five times apiece.

Since the early 1990s, Carpenter has been a very good runner on the roads, as evidenced by his 2:19 time in a sea level road marathon in 1992. But he has especially excelled on the steep, high-altitude trails that make even mountain goats stop and take a breather.

Carpenter, who turned 38 in 2002, holds course records for numerous mountain races around the world, including the Pikes Peak Ascent (2:01:06, 13.32 miles) and Pikes Peak Marathon (3:16:39, 26.2 miles). Some of his efforts border on the unthinkable, especially two of his high-altitude marathon marks. In 1995, he won the Everest SkyMarathon in 3:22:25—a race run at 17,060 feet above sea level. Three years later, he won the same race on a different course at 14,435 feet in a lung-burning 2:52:57, a time that remains the official world marathon high-altitude record.

Carpenter's uncanny desire to train harder than anyone else around is complemented by a physique built for altitude running. (His running motto is "Go out hard; when it hurts, speed up.") In 1992, he recorded an astronomically high VO^2 max—a measure of the body's ability to efficiently deliver oxygen to the muscles. His 90.2 mark is the second-highest ever recorded (only a Swedish cross-country skier posted a better mark) and approximately twice that of an average recreational athlete. It's earned him the nickname of "The Lung."

"He's the king," concedes Dave Mackey, a champion trail marathoner from Boulder, Colorado. "He's in a class all by himself."

Carpenter is also one of the founders of The Incline Club, a Manitou Springs-based running club. For more about Carpenter, visit www.skyrunner.com.

Lisa Rainsberger:
Giving Back through Coaching

In the 1980s and early 1990s, Lisa Rainsberger (then known as Lisa Weidenbach) was a world-class marathoner and one of the best road runners in the U.S. She is the last American woman to win the prestigious Boston Marathon (as of 2003), which she accomplished in 1985 with a 2:34:06 effort. Her 2:28:12 personal best time in the marathon ranked No. 8 on the all-time U.S. list as of 2002.

Rainsberger, who turned 40 in 2002, has lived and trained in many places around the U.S., but she admits her favorite place to run is in Colorado. The native of Battle Creek, Michigan, settled in Colorado Springs in 1997. She can often be seen running on the Monument Valley Trail system, Santa Fe Trail, Section 16 on Cheyenne Mountain and Barr Trail on Pikes Peak.

"We're dug in—this is home," Rainsberger says. "I'm finding, the older I get, the more time I spend on trails. It just feels better. And there are fabulous trails around Colorado Springs."

Although she finished fourth in the U.S. Olympic Trials Marathon in 1984, 1988 and 1992 (thereby missing a chance to run in the Olympics by just one place each year), she didn't let that frustration stop her from becoming one of the top road runners in U.S. history. She won numerous marathons, including Montreal (1984), Chicago (1988, 1989), Hokkaido, Japan (1990), and the Twin Cities (1993), and set a world and American record for 30k (roughly 18.6 miles) in 1986.

Since her last competitive race in 2000, Rainsberger has coached a variety of runners and triathletes ranging from first-timers to national-class athletes through Team 'N Training and Carmichael Training Systems.

"I really enjoy giving back and helping runners," she says. "It's really rewarding to see people achieve their goals and have a good time doing it."

Lisa Rainsberger is one of the most successful road runners in U.S. history.

Front Range South Running Resources

Track Facilities

The southern Front Range has several good track for speed workouts. One of the best is at Colorado College, adjacent to the Monument Valley Trail system in central Colorado Springs. Although the eight-lane, all-weather track is technically a private facility, it is open to the public under the stipulation that recreational runners use the outside lanes to reduce wear on the inner lanes. With the exception of the CC track, all of the tracks listed below are publicly owned facilities; however, each has its own rules for public usage that should be obeyed.

* Colorado College, 14 E. Cache la Poudre St., Colorado Springs. (The track at Washburn Field is located west of the school near Monument Valley Park.)
* Coronado High School, 1590 W. Fillmore St., Colorado Springs
* Cheyenne Mountain High School, 1118 W. Cheyenne Rd., Colorado Springs
* Lewis Palmer High School, 1300 Higby Dr., Monument
* Manitou Springs High School, 401 El Monte Pl., Manitou Springs
* Pueblo West High School, 661 Capistrano Dr., Pueblo
* Rampart High School, 8250 Lexington Dr., Colorado Springs

Group Runs

Colorado Running Company,

a running retailer, organizes low-key group runs on Monday, Wednesday and Friday mornings that start from its store at 833 N. Tejon St., Colorado Springs, (303) 635-3833. To make sure you won't be running alone, call the store for details a day before a run.

The Incline Club

meets on Thursday evenings and Sunday mornings for a variety of training runs prescribed by Matt Carpenter. Runners range in ability from newcomers to elite; many train for one of the three races on Pikes Peak. Visit www.inclineclub.com for details.

Pikes Peak Road Runners

is the biggest running club along the southern Front Range. It hosts a variety of group runs and races throughout the year, including the monthly 2-mile Nielson Challenge at North Monument Valley Park, Saturday morning runs at Palmer Park and a women's group run on Mondays and Wednesdays. Visit www.pprun.org for the latest info.

Southern Colorado Runners

holds several group runs during the week, including Wednesday, Saturday and Sunday mornings at the swimming pool parking lot in Pueblo's City Park for eight- to 10-mile runs at a nine-minute-mile pace. The group also holds the 10-race Prediction Series each year, a point circuit that includes races from 5k to eight miles. Visit www.socorunners.org for more details.

Triple Crown of Running

competitors meet for 45-minute training runs Tuesdays and Thursdays at Garden of the Gods from early April to early June and at the Penrose Equestrian Center (1045 W. Rio Grande St.) in Bear Creek Regional Park from early June to early July. For details, call Runners Roost at (719) 632-2633.

Running Retailers

Big 5 Sporting Goods

4330 N. Freeway, Pueblo
(719) 542-0073

Boulder Running Company

3659 Austin Bluffs Pkwy., Colorado Springs
(719) 278-3535
www.boulderrunningcompany.com

REI

1376 E. Woodmen Rd., Colorado Springs
(719) 260-1455
www.rei.com

Runners Roost

107 E. Bijou St., Colorado Springs
(719) 632-2633
www.runnersroost.com

Colorado Running Company

833 N. Tejon St., Colorado Springs
(719) 635-3833

The Danielesque Trail Runs are a pair of gnarly races held every fall at White Ranch Park in Golden.

Races and Resources

There are more than 450 running races in Colorado every year, about 300 of which are held in and around the Front Range. That gives runners of all abilities a lot of decisions to make. Which ones should you run? Start with the races listed in this section and you won't be upset.

Here are a few pointers to consider when planning your race season:

* Trail running races often have capacity limits and usually fill up earlier than road races. For example, the Pikes Peak Ascent typically reaches its limit by late spring, even though the race isn't held until mid-August.

* Racing at higher altitudes can be extremely taxing on your body, regardless of the distance. The best advice you can heed is to make sure you start slowly and hydrate early and often.

* Ultra-distance races (any race longer than a standard marathon) require an enormous amount of training. Don't sign up for the Leadville Trail 100 unless you've already completed at least a 50-mile race.

* If you're planning to run a race in the mountains, you'd be wise to arrive the night before. Getting up at the crack of dawn and driving two hours to a race isn't the best way to get your body ready to race.

* Consider running a snowshoe race to maintain your race fitness in the winter. Snowshoe running is very different than trail or road running, so be sure to practice before race day. Also, start with a 5k for your first event so you don't bite off more than you can chew.

The Best Races along Colorado's Front Range

1. Alferd Packer Trail Challenge, 13.1 miles, 26.2 miles, 39.3 miles, Littleton

Early March

www.coachweber.com

Race director Scott Weber has been holding trail races at Chatfield State Park in Littleton for many years, but none compares with this one. It's run primarily on singletrack and doubletrack trails. Although there aren't many hills, there is usually plenty of mud and every 13.1-mile lap includes two crossings of the South Platte River. In early March, the river runs cold—so cold, in fact, that there are often ice chunks floating downstream. It's no wonder the race is named after America's only convicted cannibal. Your goal should be survival, not a fast time.

2. American Discovery Trail Marathon and Relay, 26.2 miles, Palmer Lake to Colorado Springs

Early September (Labor Day)

(719) 635-3833, www.adtmarathon.com

Looking to run a fast marathon time, but don't want to pound the pavement? The ADT Marathon is a point-to-point event run primarily on hard-packed dirt trails. The course drops 1,300 feet from Palmer Lake to Colorado Springs, offering incredible views of the U.S. Air Force Academy and Pikes Peak along the way. It's one of the few official Boston Marathon qualifiers in the country run on an unpaved course.

3. Barr Mountain Trail Race, 12 miles, Manitou Springs

Mid July

(719) 685-5654, www.runpikespeak.com

This race from the base of Pikes Peak up to Barr Camp (10,200 feet) and back has developed a solid reputation since its founding in 2000 both for the spectacular scenery and the high thrill factor. The first 6 miles are a steep and grueling grind upward, while the second six are a fast and furious downhill. The race also donates a good chunk of its proceeds—more than $15,000 in 2002—to area non-profits and high schools.

The Colorado Outward Bound Relay runs through the heart of the Rocky Mountains in the peak of the golden aspen season.

4. Bolder Boulder, 10k, Boulder

Memorial Day (last Monday in May)

(303) 444-7223, www.bolderboulder.com

For anyone who runs in Colorado, this is a must-do event. One of the best road races on the planet, it annually draws about 45,000 participants. The moderately challenging course has two significant hills, but you hardly notice those with all of the spectators, bands, belly dancers and other sideline entertainment lining the course. The 2003 Bolder Boulder marked the 25th anniversary of the race, which was cofounded by 1972 Olympic marathon champion (and longtime Boulder resident) Frank Shorter. When the citizen race ends, the real action begins, as running stalwarts from around the world battle it out in men's and women's International Team Challenge in a criterium course along Folsom Street.

5. Colorado Outward Bound Relay, 170 miles, Idaho Springs to Glenwood Springs

Mid September

(888) 837-5201, www.outwardboundrelay.com

If you've never run the Colorado Outward Bound Relay, stop what you're doing and plan your entire running season around it. The camaraderie, epic fall scenery and unique adventure involved in this team running race make it an experience to remember. Each team has 10 runners and each member runs three legs (roughly 4 to 8 miles each) during a 24-hour period. (There's also a category for ultrarunning teams, in which five runners run one leg of approximately 34 miles.) The route, which crosses four high mountain passes in the heart of the Rocky Mountains, consists of paved roads, dirt trails, concrete bike paths and gravel roads. It's an ideal final speed workout for runners training for fall marathons, and it's a heck of a lot of fun. Plus you get a free pass to the Glenwood Springs Hot Springs Pool after the race.

6. Danielesque Trail Runs, 23k, 46k, Golden
Early October
(303) 271-1935, www.pmimage.com/danielesque.html
Held at White Ranch Open Space in Golden, the Danielesque Trail Runs are among the best trail races in the Front Range, if not Colorado. Why? Not only are the courses stunning, with loads of climbing and descending, but the races are run when the aspen foliage reaches its golden peak and they offer excellent aid-station support and lots of postrace goodies. Plus, they're a tribute race in honor of Daniel Rosenfeld, a dedicated Boulder ultrarunner who died in 2000. Sign up early, because there's a strict 75-runner limit.

7. Georgetown to Idaho Springs Half Marathon, 13.1 miles, Georgetown
Mid August
(303) 694-2030, www.bkbltd.com
One of the classic Front Range races, the Georgetown to Idaho Springs Half Marathon is a mostly downhill 13.1-mile race on the frontage roads along I-70. Remember the phrase "mostly downhill" when you get to about mile 9 or 10 and it feels like you're running uphill. Because of the major descent between the two mountain towns, many runners start notoriously fast and hit the wall well before Idaho Springs. If you can pace yourself and run an even race, you can easily run the fastest half-marathon time of your life.

8. Horsetooth Half Marathon and Relay, 13.1 miles, Fort Collins
Mid April
(970) 493-4675, www.footoftherockies.com
An out-and-back race that begins and ends at Colorado State's Hughes Stadium, the Horsetooth Half is one of the annual rites of spring for Front Range runners. It's a challenging road run, especially when it comes to the infamous "Dam Hill" at mile 7. One of the oldest continuously run races in Colorado, the Horsetooth Half will celebrate its 30th anniversary in 2004. In recent years, the top three finishers in each age category have received pieces of handmade pottery from a local artist.

Pro athlete Eric Scwartz cruises to victory in the 2003 Runnin' of the Green Lucky 7k in Denver.

9. Komen Race for the Cure, 5k, Denver

Early October

(303) 744-2088, www.raceforthecure-denver.com

There are more than 50 Race for the Cure events in the U.S. every year (including events in Colorado Springs and Greeley), but only a few are bigger or more remarkable than this event in Denver. It's part of a massive fund-raising event for the Komen Foundation, an organization working to eradicate breast cancer. For some participants it's a celebration of life and a triumph over cancer; for others it's a tribute to loved ones lost to the disease. The Denver race is an awe-inspiring event that typically draws 50,000 to 60,000 runners and walkers. The race is held on a fast, flat course in downtown Denver, but you'll get more inspiration being there than you will from your finishing time.

10. Pikes Peak Ascent and Marathon, 13.4 miles, 26.2 miles, Manitou Springs

Mid August

(719) 473-2625, www.pikespeakmarathon.org

These classic Colorado races have drawn runners from around the world for decades. No other race in Colorado can match the satisfaction of running up (and down, if you choose to run the whole marathon) the majestic 14,110-foot peak just outside of Colorado Springs. Some runners do it once and savor it for a lifetime, while others mark time by doing it year after year. Whether you're an elite speed-ster or a back-of-the-packer, you can't find a better race to test your physical, emotional and spiritual makeup.

Other Front Range Races

BKB Road Races
Throughout the year
(303) 694-2030, www.bkbltd.com/calendar.htm

Boulder Backroads Marathon, 13.1 miles, 26.2 miles, Boulder
Late September
(303) 939-9661, www.boulderbackroads.com

Boulder Distance Carnival, 12.5k, 25k, Boulder
Late April
(303) 786-9255, www.boulderrunningcompany.com

Canine Classic, 5k, 10k, Boulder (dogs permitted)
Third Sunday in April
(303) 939-9661, bouldermarathon@mindspring.com

Cherry Creek Sneak, 5k, 5 miles, Denver
Late April
(303) 798-7028, www.cherrycreeksneak.com

Cinco Cinco 5k, Fort Collins
Early May
(970) 224-9114, www.runnersroostftcollins.com

Coal Creek Cross Country Challenge, 5.7 miles, Louisville
Mid October
(303) 791-3384

Coopersmith's Half Marathon, 13.1 miles, Fort Collins
Early October
(970) 493-1305, www.footoftherockies.com

Cottonwood Classic, 5k, Thornton
Mid May
(303) 694-2030, www.bkbltd.com

The trails around the Boulder Reservoir play host to numerous races, including the Boulder Distance Carnival in late April.

CU Kickoff Classic, 5k, Boulder
Labor Day (first Monday in September)
(303) 492-8776, www.boulderroadrunners.org

Easy Street Marathon, 26.2 miles, Fort Collins
Early October
(970) 493-1305, www.footoftherockies.com

Eldorado Springs Cure Run, 4 miles, Eldorado Springs
Mid August
(303) 449-7624

Erie Erie, 5k, 10k, Erie
Late October
www.active.com

Firecracker 5k, 10k, Colorado Springs
July 4
(719) 635-8803, www.csgrandprix.com

Firecracker 5k, Fort Collins
July 4
(970) 493-4675, www.footoftherockies.com

Fire Hydrant 5k, Fort Collins (dogs permitted)
Mid May
(970) 224-9114, www.runnersroostftcollins.com

Freedom Run, 5k, Evegreen
July 4
(303) 694-2030, www.bkbltd.com

Frostbite 5-miler, Pueblo
Early February
(719) 543-5151

Frosty Trail Challenge, 12.5k, 25k, 50k, Littleton
Early February
www.coachweber.com

Garden of the Gods 5k, 5 miles, Colorado Springs
Early May
(719) 635-8803, www.csgrandprix.com

Garden of the Gods 10-Mile Run, Colorado Springs
Early June
(719) 473-2625, www.pikespeakmarathon.org

Greenwood Goosechase, 5k, 10k, Greenwood Village
Mid June
(303) 486-1555, www.gvchamber.com/goosechase.asp

High Five Road Race, 5 miles, Boulder
Early October
(303) 492-8776, www.boulderroadrunners.org

Highline Canal Run, 5k, 10k, Littleton
Mid May
(303) 798-7515, www.sspr.org

Horsetooth Mountain Trail Run, 8.5 miles, Fort Collins
Mid June
(970) 224-9114, www.runnersroostftcollins.com

Jingle Bell Run, 5k, Denver
Early December
(303) 694-2030, www.bkbltd.com

Joe Colton's Off-Road Adventure Run, 1 mile, 5k, 10 miles, Rollinsville
Late July
(303) 258-7113

Littleton Stride, 5k, Littleton
Mid March
(303) 694-2030, www.bkbltd.com

Lory Trail Run, 9.5 miles, Fort Collins
Early May
(970) 221-0080

Lyons River Run, 5k, Lyons
Late June
(303) 823-8250

Mile High City Marathon, 13.1 miles, 26.2 miles, Denver
Mid September
(303) 375-8121, www.milehighcitymarathon.com

Mile High United Way Turkey Trot, 4 miles, Denver
Thanksgiving Day
(303) 694-2030, www.bkbltd.com

Mt. Evans Ascent, 14 miles, Evergreen
Early June
(970) 389-4838, www.racingunderground.com

Mt. Falcon Trail Run, 8 miles, Morrison
Mid June
(303) 674-6441

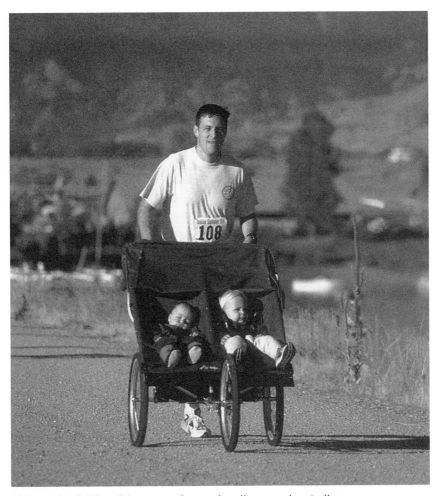

Find out ahead of time if the race you're running allows running strollers.

Neder Nederland 5k, Nederland
Early September
(303) 258-0258

Nielson Challenge, 2 miles, Colorado Springs
Every month
(719) 633-2055, www.pprrun.org

Pearl Street Mile, 1 mile, Boulder
Late July
(303) 413-7316, www.gettingthere.com/calendar

The Screamin' Snowman Snowshoe Races at Eldora Mountain Resort in Nederland are some of the best in the state.

Resolution Run, 5k, Denver
December 31
(303) 635-2815, www.emgcolorado.com

Race for Research, 5k, Denver
Late August
(303) 694-2030, www.bkbltd.com

Really Greeley Run, 5k, Greeley
Late July
(970) 356-6775, www.greeleydowntown.com

Runnin' of the Green Lucky 7k, Denver
Mid March
(303) 694-2030, www.bkbltd.com

Screamin' Snowman Snowshoe Races, 5k, 10k, Eldora
Early February
(303) 527-1798, www.racingunderground.com

Slacker Half Marathon, 13.1 miles, Loveland Ski Area to Georgetown
Late June
(303) 519-0357, www.bkbltd.com

Spring Runoff, 5k, 10k, 10 miles, Pueblo
Early March
(800) 945-2464, www.chieftain.com/springrunoff/

Stadium Stampede, 5k, Denver
Late June
(303) 694-2030, www.bkbltd.com

Sunrise Stampede, 2 miles, 10k, Longmont
Early June
(303) 449-2825

Thanksgiving Day Run, 4 miles, Fort Collins
Thanksgiving Day
(970) 482-0551

Three Sisters Trail Race, 10k, Evergreen
Mid July
(303) 674-6441

Wheat Ridge Farmers 5000, 5k, Wheat Ridge
Mid September
(303) 982-7695, www.farmers5000.com

Other Colorado Races

Autumn Color Run, 13.1 miles, Buena Vista
Mid September
(719) 395-6612, www.fourteener.net

Beaver Creek Snowshoe Series, 5k, 10k, Beaver Creek
(Four dates, December through March)
(970) 476-6797, www.bcsnowshoe.com

Breckenridge Crest Trail Races, 5 miles, 10 miles, 24.5 miles, Breckenridge
First Sunday in September
(970) 453-6422, www.boec.org

Collegiate Peaks Trail Runs, 25 miles, 50 miles, Buena Vista
Early May
(719) 395-6612, www.fourteener.net

Frisco Snowshoe Series, 5k, Frisco
Late January
(303) 635-2815, www.emgcolorado.com

Imogene Pass Run, 17.1 miles, Ouray to Telluride
Early September
(719) 633-2055, www.csbservices.com

Leadville Trail 100, 100 miles, Leadville
Mid August
(719) 486-3502, www.leadvilletrail100.com

Leadville Trail Marathon, 26.2 miles, Leadville
Early July
(719) 486-3502, www.leadvilletrail100.com

San Juan Solstice Trail Run, 50 miles, Lake City
Late June
(970) 944-2269, www.lakecity50.com

Scott Boulbol and Taz make sure they follow the leash laws whenever they run on trails.

Steamboat Running Series, Steamboat Springs
May to October
www.runningseries.com

Swift Skeedaddle Snowshoe Races, 3k, 10k, Silverthorne
Early January to early March
(970) 389-4838, www.racingunderground.com

Vail Trail Running Series
May to September
(970) 479-2280, www.vailrec.com

Largest Races on the Front Range

Race	Runners*
Race for the Cure 5k, Denver	54,000
Bolder Boulder 10k, Boulder	45,000
Cherry Creek Sneak 5k, 5 miles, Denver	12,000
Mile High United Way Turkey Trot, Denver	8,000
Race for the Cure 5k, Colorado Springs	7,500
Runnin' of the Green Lucky 7k, Denver	4,000
Georgetown to Idaho Springs Half-Marathon	2,800
Boulder Backroads Marathon, Half-Marathon	2,500
Littleton Stride 5k, 10k, Littleton	2,225
Jingle Bell Run, 5k, Denver	1,975
Freedom Run 5k, Evergreen	1,550
Pikes Peak Ascent, 13.3 miles, Manitou Springs	1,500
Evergreen Town Race, 5k, 10k, Evergreen	1,306
Fort Collins Old Town Marathon, Half-Marathon	1,200
Stadium Stampede 5k, Denver	1,200
Garden of the Gods, 10 miles, Colorado Springs	1,100
Race for Research 5k, Denver	1,100
Mile High City Marathon, Half-Marathon and 5k, Denver	1,050
Outward Bound Relay, Idaho Springs to Glenwood Springs	1,000

* approximate figures supplied by race directors, news reports

Feel the need for speed? There is a race almost every weekend somewhere along the Front Range.

Colorado Coaching Services

Anaerobic Management
Fort Collins/Front Range
www.anaerobic.net

Anthem Fit Training Program
Boulder/Denver
(303) 444-6011, www.anthemcampus.com

Bolder Boulder Training Program
Boulder
(303) 444-RACE, www.bolderboulder.com

Boulder/Denver Fit
Boulder/Denver
(303) 546-6331, www.bouldefit.com

Boulder Striders/Running Republic
Boulder
(303) 579-0870, kwazulu11@msn.com

Carmichael Training Systems
Colorado Springs/Front Range
(719) 635-0645, www.trainright.com

Run Fit
Boulder/Denver
(303) 440-1220, runfitdan@juno.com

Team in Training
Front Range
(303) 984-2110, www.teamintraining.org/rm

Colorado Running Camps

Altitude Training Clinics
Leadville, Colorado
(888) 486-3155

Colorado High Altitude Camps
Woodland Park, Colorado
(719) 591-9316

Running Wild
Boulder, Colorado; Reserve, New Mexico
(303) 263-1523

Women's Quest Fitness Retreats
Winter Park, Colorado
(303) 545-9295, www.womensquest.com

Running Resources

All American Trail Running Association
Colorado Springs, Colorado
www.trailrunner.com

American Running Association
Bethesda, Maryland
(800) 776-2732, www.americanrunning.org

American Ultrarunning Association
Morristown, New Jersey
(973) 898-1261, www.americanultra.org

Boulder Running
Boudler, Colorado
www.BoulderRunning.com
greg@boulderrunning.com.

Colorado Running Guide
Boulder, Colroado
www.coloradorunningguide.com

Road Runners Club of America
Alexandria, Virginia
(703) 836-0558, www.rrca.org

Runner's World magazine
Emmaus, Pennsylvania
(800) 666-2828, www.runnersworld.com

Running USA
Santa Barbara, California
(805) 964-0608, www.runningusa.com

Run the Planet
Seattle, Washington
www.runtheplanet.com

Trail Runner magazine
Carbondale, Colorado
(970) 704-1442, www.trailrunnermag.com

USA Track & Field
Indianapolis, Indiana
(317) 261-0500, www.usatf.org

Front Range Triathlons/ Multi-sport Races

Winter Triathlon Series, Tabernash
December to March
www.mountain-quest.com

Looking to revitalize your running? Sign up for a triathlon this summer.

Barking Dog Duathlon, Keenesburg
Early May
(303) 642-7917, www.racingunderground.com

Boulder Stroke and Stride Series
Thursdays in Summer
www.5430tri.com

Longmont Triathlon, Longmont
Early June
(303) 651-8404

Rattlesnake Triathlon, Aurora
Mid June, Mid July, Mid August
(303) 885-8122

Greeley Triathlon, Greeley
Mid June
(720) 299-6941, www.greeleytriathlon.com

Loveland Lake to Lake Triathlon
Late June
(970) 669-6372, www.lovelandlaketolake.com

Saturn Triathlon, Palmer Lake
Early July
(719) 632-3933, www.timberlinetiming.com

5430 Triathlon, Boulder
Mid July
www.5430tri.com

Boulder Peak Triathlon, Boulder
Early August
(303) 380-9155, www.boulderpeak.com

Harvest Moon Long Course Triathlon/Duathlon, Aurora
Early September
(303) 642-7917, www.racingunderground.com

Front Range Triathlon Clubs

Boulder Triathlon Club, Boulder
(720) 480-4600, www.bouldertriathlonclub.org

Dave Scott's MultiSport Club, Boulder
(303) 786-7184

Northern Colorado Triathlon Club, Fort Collins
(970) 225-0212

Pikes Peak Triathlon Club, Colorado Springs
(719) 481-2337

Team 365, Boulder
(303) 449-4800, www.team365.net

The Stroke and Stride race series features a 1-mile swim and a 5k run on Thursday nights at the Boulder Reservoir. Visit www.5430tri.com for details.

Tri Altitude Multi-Sport Club, Highlands Ranch

(303) 471-0512

Women's Triathlon Club, Boulder

(303) 554-8857

About the Author

On a visit to Colorado in 1988, author Brian Metzler ran up Flagstaff Mountain in Boulder and changed his view of running forever. He moved to Boulder shortly thereafter and has been running the roads and trails of the Front Range ever since. A former middle-distance track runner in high school and college, he is the founding editor of *Trail Runner: The Magazine of Running Adventure* and *Adventure Sports Magazine* and has written about running for *The (Boulder) Daily Camera, The Denver Post, The Chicago Tribune* and *Outside* magazine. He has competed in dozens of Colorado races since 1992, ranging from the Bolder Boulder 10k to the Leadville Trail 100, and has served advisory roles with the All American Trail Running Association and USA Track & Field's Mountain/Ultra/Trail Running Council.

One of his favorite adventure runs was a 48-mile jaunt from Winter Park to Boulder in September 2001, when the autumnal foliage of the aspen trees had reached its golden peak. He ran up and over Rollins Pass and along Jenny Creek Trail and then followed Magnolia Road down into Boulder, stopping only once for a quick snack in Nederland. He admits he never would have been able to finish it without the support of his wife, Pam, who followed along on a mountain bike with extra water and a bevy of good humor. The couple lives in Boulder with their daughter, Lucy, and Boggs, their three-year-old Wheaten Terrier and frequent running partner.